CSC-105 BC

(Before Commodore)

By: Marc Lipman

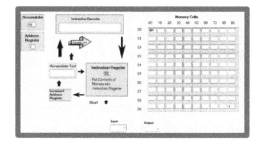

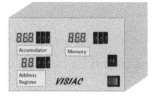

An introduction to computers and computer science in a simplistic way
with the past history and future history of computers.

Table of Contents

Forward

As a software developer / development manager for over 30 years and a college professor for almost 25, I have seen amazing developments in the field of computer science. Trying to explain modern computer concepts is a daunting task. The modern textbook is so complicated that many (or most) readers find the material too difficult to comprehend (notice I used the word "comprehend" instead of a simpler word).

This book attempts to alleviate (notice I used a more complicated word again) the situation by describing the concepts from a 1970's perspective. From this point on we are going back in time (however, as required, I will jump back and forth in time).

Figuring out how much computer science stuff to put in this book involved the same approach that I would take in creating a statue of a horse. I start with a block of granite and remove everything that doesn't look like a horse.

Since the purpose of this book is to explain ideas and concepts, If you find some detail that is incorrect, don't write a letter stating that the author doesn't know what he is talking about (even if he doesn't).

Introduction

Welcome to CSC-105 BC. I'm your instructor, Marc Lipman. This non-class / non-textbook is going to teach you about computer concepts based on the current technology (as of the current time - the 1970's). Since I keep up with latest technology, learn about what is now being developed and am somewhat clairvoyant, I will occasionally tell you about the near future (5 or 10 years from now) and make predictions about what we may see the distant future (the mid 2010's), and maybe even farther. These future items are covered later in this book – But don't peek!

Constant evolution of computers and digital devices. New and improved computers and digital devices are coming out every year (sometimes One of my favorite non-fiction books is about dinosaurs. It talks about them from an evolutionary perspective; the smaller ones from the Triassic, to the Brontosaurus of the Jurassic, huge and slow, to the Triceratops of the Cretaceous, much smaller, but faster and more powerful with 4 foot long horns. Computers have evolved in the same way. The Univac 1219 of the fifties was slow and moderately sized (by today's standards). Evolution produced the IBM 360/370 series, much larger and more powerful, and then servers the size of a refrigerator with many times that power.

To some readers this book may be very much like a steer: a point here, a point there, and a lot of bull in between.

Some themes that will permeate this book are:

- more often than that). It may not be a good idea to wait for a better one. An even better one will be coming the following year.
- One size fits all – **NOT!** As an example: If I asked 20 students what printer would be best for their needs, I might get 20 different answers.
- Computers and digital devices becoming a part of every aspect of business and personal life. In the 70's who would imagine that your refrigerator would have a built-in camera and be able to talk to your phone?
- One feature of a device should not be used to judge the applicability of that device to your needs. A camera with a 20 Megapixel sensor but a mediocre lens is no substitute for a 10 Megapixel one with a great lens.

Treat this book like a smorgasbord. Rather than a 5 course meal where you are expected to eat the whole thing, you can pick and choose what you like. If some area doesn't interest you, just go on to the next one.

Let's start simple, the ABC's (01000001, 01000010, 01000011's for those of you who know binary). As a hardware model, I will be using the VISIAC - a simple home computer emulation (a program that looks to a user like the original object) based on the CARDIAC - a folded cardboard "computer." More about these will be explained in the chapter about CARDIAC / VISIAC.

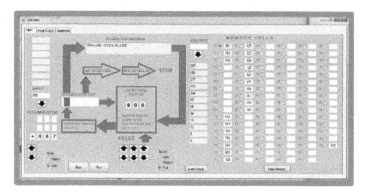

Figure 1: The Cardiac (C 1968)

Sometimes there will be a subject that is beyond the scope of this book. If so, I will state: "This subject is beyond the scope of this book." Sometimes there will be a subject that I don't understand. If so, I will state: "This subject is beyond the scope of this book"

Section 1: The Present (the 70's)

1: What is a computer?

A computer is an electronic data processing device that takes input and produces output. All computers use 4 basic operations plus communications:

- **Input:** What goes into the computer system

- **Processing:** The manipulation a computer does to transform data into information.

- **Storage:**

    - **Primary storage,** or **memory,** is temporary storage for data waiting to be processed.

    - **Secondary storage** is permanent storage: media such as magnetic tape or hard disk drives.

- **Output:** What comes out—the results of processing, such as computer cards, screen output, or printouts.

- **Communications:** Sending and receiving data to and from other digital devices.

There are general purpose computers, those that we can program to do business or personal operations, and special purpose computers, those that are made for a specific function.

Here's an example of a special purpose computer – a greeting card of the future. You say something into it and send it to Aunt

Mary. She opens it and it sings "Happy birthday to you, Aunt Mary." It meets the definition of a computer. You sang into it. That's input. It processed your voice and saved it. That's processing and storage. When she opened it up, it sang to her. That's output. Another example is a current system – The Safeguard Anti-Missile System. It was specifically designed to detect enemy missiles and fire missiles to intercept them. Its multi-processor system includes high-performance hardware, radar controllers, and a real-time operating system. It didn't play computer games or do your taxes or read your E-Mail.

The concept of "Data into Information" is important. Raw numbers do not mean much to us. But put them into a graph or table and they become meaningful. Imagine the world of the future where we will be able to also use color, pictures, sounds and even video to make our information more understandable.

Take the Didgeridoo, an Australian aboriginal musical instrument. I could describe one to you. But if I could also show you a picture of one and even play the sound of one, you would understand it a lot better.

Figure 2: A Didgeridoo

As another example, take the offer I made to the students at the beginning of one of my courses. I offered to let a student do a take-home final, given one week. Whatever grade they got would be it for the course. I got a few raised hands. Then I explained that the final was in encrypted binary. The hands immediately went down.

Hardware / Software

Computers need both hardware and software to run. Hardware is the circuitry needed to process the instructions. It also includes the case, the keyboard, the screen, and the power supply. Software is the programs – the instructions that tell the computer exactly what to do. They have evolved together. Faster hardware with more memory allows us to develop more sophisticated software.

Sizes of computers

Computers come in several sizes. At the top are Supercomputers, very expensive, very large and very fast. For example, the Cray-1 Supercomputer runs four and a half times faster than a mainframe and only weighs about five and a half tons. Its speed is 160 MFLOPS (160 million floating-point instructions per second). We don't have to know what that means. I am only stating that because my view of the future shows a supercomputer of 2017 with a speed of 93 TFLOPS (a TFLOP is a million times faster than a MFLOP).

Next we have Mainframe computers. As an example, the IBM/360 is a fast computer used by large companies for processing such items as payroll, accounting and inventory management. These computers are expensive – hundreds of thousands of dollars (remember, the price of a gallon of gas today is 27 cents), require an air conditioned environment, and can perform complicated processing.

There are smaller, less expensive computers such as the PDP-11's, a series of 16-bit minicomputers sold by Digital Equipment Corporation (DEC) starting in 1970. Their cost of about $11,000 is much less than that of a Mainframe.

For years any kind of computer was beyond the reach of individuals. Now for the first time we can buy our own computer, the Altair 8000. It is inexpensive ($439 as a kit) and is designed for people who just want a computer. I expect that soon people will be able to buy their own "useful" computer. Since they will be fruitful, they may even name one after a fruit like an apple.

When I use these terms I am careful to use relative ones. My view of the future shows that the PC's of the 2000's will be more powerful than the mainframes of today.

For this book we have an alternative to the ALTAIR, the VISIAC. Although it is simple, almost a toy, we can learn computer concepts from it. But first let's start with some basics.

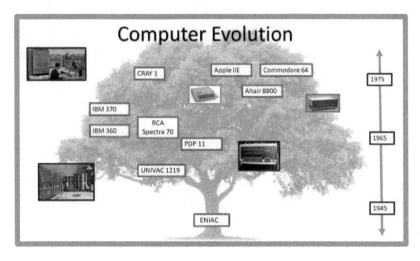

Figure 3: Computer Evolution

Binary Arithmetic

Computers use binary arithmetic. In early elementary school we learned about decimal arithmetic. Decimal arithmetic has 10 digits, 0 to 9. We know that if a number is bigger than 9 we must use the 10's column and if the number is bigger than 99, we must use the 100's column and so forth.

In binary arithmetic we only have 2 digits, a "0" and a "1." Therefore, if the number is bigger than 1 we must use the next column (you guessed it, the 2's column). The following column is the 4's column followed by the 8's column and so forth. When we add numbers if there is a carry, it goes into the next column (remember, there is a carry if the number is bigger than 1). Computers use binary because their electronics work with circuits that are on or off – a "1" or a '0."

Powers of 2

2^0	1
2^1	2
2^2	4
2^3	8
2^4	16
2^5	32
2^6	64
2^7	128
2^8	256

Table 1: Powers of 2

With a byte (8 bits) we could have an unsigned number as big as 511 (add up all the numbers in the second column of table 1). With 2 bytes we could have a signed number (plus or minus) between -32,168[1] and 32,167.

Now you try it: What is the decimal equivalent of "01010100" on binary? Answer:

84

But there's more.   Programmers don't like working with a lot of digits. A byte (8 bits) has eight binary digits, and computers that use 32 bit words require 32 1's and 0's. That's a lot of 1's and 0's. So they use a numbering system called hexadecimal (hex for short). This numbering system has 16 digits, "0" to "9" AND "A" to "F". After the 1's column we now have the 16's column and the 256's column. The largest digit (the "F") is equal to 15 (1 + 2 + 4 + 8). Therefore we can represent four binary digits as one hex digit. In the following table we see the addition of two numbers in each numbering system.

Decimal	Hex	Binary
1447	5A7	010110100111
+ 347	+15B	+000101011010
=1494	=702	=011100000010

Table 2: Numbering Systems

Sizing things up

In our contemporary life there many units of measurements: length, weight, volume, and pressure, both traditional and

---

[1] This is because computers used two's complement arithmetic, which is beyond the scope of this book.

metric. In the computer world we only have a couple: data storage and data transfer rates. The standard for data storage is the byte. A byte is 8 bits. A computer is able to access any piece of data in its memory by specifying its byte address. Whether the computer can store 64 thousand bytes or 4 billion bytes, its CPU can access any byte by specifying its address. In our regular world we have centimeters, meters and kilometers because we have many different ranges of size. The same holds true for our computer world. We have:

- A bit: A binary digit, either a "0" or a "1".
- A byte: 8 bits
- A kilobyte: 1,024 bytes (roughly a thousand)
- A megabyte 1,048,576 bytes (roughly a million)
- A gigabyte: 1,073,741,824 bytes (roughly a billion)
- A terabyte: 1,099,511,627,776 bytes (roughly a thousand billion)
- A petabyte: 1,125,899,906,842,624 bytes (roughly a million billion)

Because we are using binary with powers of two, the units of measure do not exactly correspond to our decimal units of measure, although they are close.

Similarly we have measurements for data transfer. Data transfer may be data going to and from our storage devices, to and from our input/output devices, and to and from the Internet. Because some of these transfers are bits at a time, not bytes at a time, we have to be careful of confusing terminology. A Kbps and a KBps are NOT the same. A small "b" is bits per second. A capital "B" is bytes per second.

Digital and Analog

Up until the days of computers, everything was analog. In the old style thermometers the level of the column of mercury was directly proportional to the temperature. If your eyes were good, you could tell the temperature to a fraction of a degree. Clocks used sand, shadows, and gears. Record players used grooves cut into plastic. Cameras used plastic sheets with chemicals on them. The gadget on the right is a slide rule. It can do multiplication, division, logarithms, and trig calculations simply by moving the slide (no batteries required).

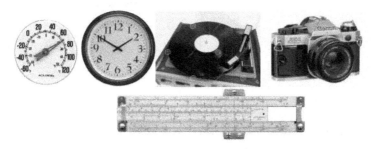

Here are some examples of analog devices:

Then engineers figured out that they could design digital devices that displayed the information as text or numbers rather than the movement of a dial or the height of a column of mercury. For some this makes the information more readable (a matter of preference).

Here are some digital devices:

Electrical signals can be analog or digital. In music, the signal going to the speakers is in an analog form. The higher the voltage, the louder the sound; the closer together the waves, the higher the frequency of the sound.

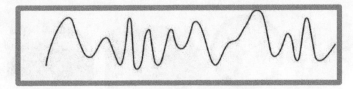

Figure 4: An analog signal

Digital electrical signals consist of voltage and no voltage (ones and zeros). The signal may not contain as much detail as an analog signal (many audiophiles prefer records), but as long as the receiver on the other end can tell the difference between a one and a zero, the signal will be received with no loss of data. Also, the signal can also include information to tell the receiving end whether the information was received correctly.

Here is an example: suppose we added up the numerical values of the bytes sent (e.g. 7,468) and added another byte with the number -7,468. When the data is received at the other end, and we add up the values, we should get a zero. If we don't, something is wrong! This approach will work whether the signal is coming from your nearby microwave tower or from Pluto.

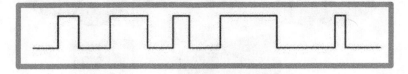

Figure 5: A digital signal

Digital Circuits

Computers and digital devices use digital circuits for processing and storing data, those that use the concept of "on" and "off." A small section of a hard disk may be magnetized one way or the other way. A CD or DVD surface may have shiny or dull segments. A transistor can either be conducting current (a zero) or not conducting current (a one). The following figure shows a simple transistor circuit. There are 5 transistors and 7 resisters (the squiggly lines).The ⏚ symbol is for a ground. I could make this circuit by buying these devices and wiring them together on a circuit board. Notice that there are 4 inputs (A to D) and 2 outputs (NOR or OR). It uses 5 volts. If we put a voltage on **A** or B or C or D, the corresponding transistor conducts current. This keeps the final transistor from conducting current and makes the OR output a one. Thus we have what we call an OR gate. The **OR** output is a one (true) if A is true or B is true or C is true or D is true (NOR is simply NOT OR).

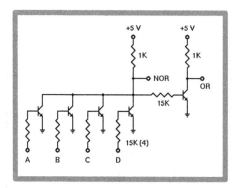

Figure 6: A Digital Logic Gate

When designing computer circuits, we use symbols to represent these kind of circuits. We call these logic gates. There are only a few logic gate types needed to design digital circuits.

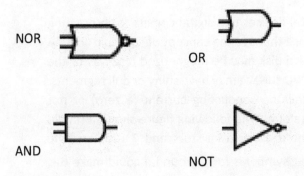

NOR

OR

AND

NOT

Table 3: Logic Gate Symbols

The following diagram shows how an OR Gate works.

Input	Output
0000	0
0001	1
0010	1
...	...
1111	1

Table 4: The "OR" Logic diagram

The following diagram shows how an AND Gate works.

Input	Output

0000	0
0001	0
0010	0
...	...
1111	1

Table 5: The "AND" Logic diagram

Let's build a simple circuit using an OR Gate and an AND Gate. Note we use these logic symbols instead of drawing the circuit symbols.

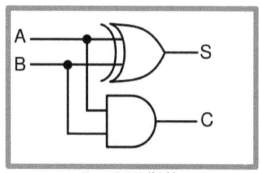

Figure 4: A Half Adder

If we put a lot of these together we would have a circuit that adds two binary numbers (8 of these to add the contents of two one byte registers.

We need one more kind of circuit, the flip-flop. Once you set it, it stays that way until you reset it. The accumulator (a register in the CPU) uses flip-flops (one for each bit) to retain the information as long as the CPU has power. There is also a toggle flip-flop. It changes its state (off to on or on to off) whenever its input is pulsed.

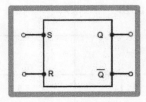

Figure 5: A Set / Reset Flip-flop

How do we make these circuits?

In the 1940's the designers used vacuum tubes and relays (the silicon transistor would not be available until 1954). Vacuum tubes are big, use a lot of power, produce a lot of heat and burn out easily.

Figure 6: A vacuum tube computer circuit

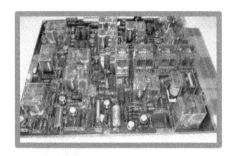

Figure 7: A relay computer circuit

Critics of the ENIAC computer said that if a vacuum tube failed, by the time they found it and replaced it, another would fail, and the computer would never work! In reality they soon were able to limit the failures to a bad vacuum tube every couple of days.

With the advent of the transistor, all that changed. By using transistors, computers could be smaller, faster, cheaper and more reliable. Discrete transistors gave way to integrated circuits. The Integrated Circuit (IC) was a way of putting a large number of transistors and resistors on a single silicon chip. Integrated circuits gave way to Large Scale Integration (10,000 transistors or more on a chip). We are still using the same logic circuits as in the 50's, but on a vastly smaller (more compact) size.

Figure 8: Evolution of processor hardware

Parts of a computer

The heart of a computer is the Central Processing Unit (CPU). The CPU is the unit that reads the instructions from the memory and executes them. The Intel 8080 microprocessor (used in small computers and devices such as cash registers) has about 50 instructions in its instruction set, the IBM/360 mainframe computers over 150, and at least double that for the newer computers.

With these instructions, programmers can make this computer do something useful (remember, without any programs in it a computer can't do anything). Why do we need all these instructions? That's easy, speed and the ability to do more calculations with fewer instructions (saving memory). Here's an example. With only the ability to add 8 bits at a time, you would have to execute 4 instructions to add a big number. If your CPU had an instruction to add 4 bytes at a time, your program would run faster and need less memory.

Arithmetic with fractions and large numbers requires even more processing, Adding 6.07×10^7 to 5.937×10^6 requires a number of steps. If we could build circuits to do that, we could make our computer run much faster (floating point arithmetic). Now you may see why supercomputer speed is measured in floating point instructions per second (FLOPS).

For learning purposes let's consider the least number of instructions in a CPU needed to design a program. The VISIAC CPU is a single-accumulator single-address machine. Thus each instruction operates optionally on a single memory location and the accumulator. Following is the instruction set from the VISIAC:

OP CODES		
Code	Abr.	Meaning
0	INP	Input
1	CLA	Clear & Add
2	Add	Add
3	TAC	Test Accum. Contents
4	SFT	Shift
5	OUT	Output
6	STO	Store
7	SUB	Subtract
8	JMP	Jump
9	HRS	Halt & Reset

Figure 9: The VISIAC Instruction Set

You notice that there are only ten instructions[2] as opposed to the hundreds of instructions in the IBM/370 Mainframe (a more expensive model might have more instructions). A bigger more complicated instruction repertoire requires more hardware (circuits). More hardware costs more money.

But, don't despair, there's Moore's Law. Gordon Moore, the co-founder of Fairchild Semiconductor and Intel, made the observation that the number of transistors in a dense integrated

---

[2] See Appendix 3 for a description of what these instructions do

circuit doubles approximately every year and a half. This affects both the power of the CPU and the size of memory modules (RAM).

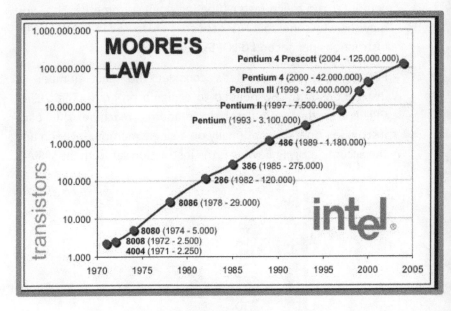

Figure 10: Moore's Law

Thus without more cost we can produce a faster processor. Here's an example of what more transistors can do. Remember our adder circuit. When we add decimal numbers, we can't do the tens column until we do the ones column since that may produce a carry. The same holds true for the hundreds column and so forth. In binary arithmetic we have the same problem. But suppose we added a circuit to calculate the carry for all the columns at once (we'll call this a "look-ahead carry chain"). Now the computer can do addition faster.

The CPU has a number of registers to hold data for the CPU to work with. Some are used by the CPU for its processing such as the address register and the instruction register. In addition there are a number of general-purpose registers available to work with the data. As an example, instructions may tell the CPU to load the contents of memory address 23 into the "A" register, add the contents of memory address 53 to it and store the result in memory address 54. The VISIAC only has one general purpose register. Modern computers have over a dozen.

Let's use a calculator analogy. Most calculators have a display that only shows one number with about 8 digits. If you want to save this number for a later calculation, you have to save it on a piece of paper. Later you have to enter that number back into the calculator. This is like the program having to store the contents of the accumulator in memory and later load it back into the accumulator.

Computers also need storage. There are two types, primary Storage and Secondary Storage.

In a modern computer Primary Storage is referred to as random access memory (RAM). Each byte (8 bits) in RAM can be accessed by the CPU by specifying its address. A byte in RAM can hold an instruction (or part of an instruction), a character ("A","Z","3","-", etc.), a part of a picture, or a part of a sound or music. Modern computer memory is volatile. That means that all its contents is lost if the power goes off. Thus, data should be copied to Secondary Storage as required.

In the old days (the fifties) RAM was made of tiny magnetic cores (donuts) that could be magnetized one way or the other – a "1" or a "0". They were slow, large and expensive, but didn't lose their values when power was shut off. Sometimes we old timers still mention "core memory."

Figure 11: Core memory and an 8 GB SD Card

In addition computers have secondary storage. While not as fast as primary storage (RAM), its cost per byte is much cheaper AND it is non-volatile (it does NOT lose its contents when power goes off). Early computers used tape drives. They looked like the reel-to-reel recorders used for music, only the size of a refrigerator. The tape you see below could hold 6,250 bytes per inch of tape.

Figure 12: A nine-track tape drive and tape

Since they were "serial" devices, you had to "fast-forward" them if the data you needed was near the end of the tape (and rewind it before you could remove the reel from the drive).

With the invention of the hard disk, this was changed. Just like with a phonograph record, you can get to a spot on the disk just by moving the arm and waiting for the platter to rotate to the right sector. To make a higher capacity disk, just add more platters.

The speed, capacity and cost of hard drives has improved over the years. Now a 300 Megabyte drive is no larger than a washing machine. To switch disk cartridges you open the lid, pull out the one inside and replace it with the new one.

Figure 13: A disk drive and disk cartridge

There are also floppy disks. They are an eight inch square (that's right!) flexible magnetic disk in a thin cardboard enclosure. They hold 180 thousand bytes of data per side. They are useful for tasks like storing instructions needed for running a high-speed line printer. I speculate that in the future they may be able to create a smaller one, perhaps 5 ¼ inches, and maybe even one 3 ½ inches. That technology may even enable one to hold as much as 1.44 Megabytes.

Figure 14: Floppy disks

All general purpose computers have the ability to input data from some source(s) and output the processed data. Mainframe computers generally use punched cards for input and high-speed printers for output. They are called line printers because they print one line (120 or 132 columns) at a time. In one type, a metal chain containing all the characters spins horizontally around a set of hammers. When the desired character lines up at the proper position, a tiny hammer hits the paper into the ribbon and onto the character in the chain. When all the characters for that line have been printed, the printer advances the paper to the next line. Line printers are fast but noisy.

Punched cards were first used to tabulate the 1890 census data since they realized that without them it would take ten years to process the data (time for the next census). Hollerith started the Tabulating Machine Company, which later became IBM.

Figure 15: Card Reader/Punch, Line Printer and TTY

Minicomputers can also use keyboards for input. A computer terminal is a device with a keyboard for input and a printer or CRT (Cathode Ray Tube) screen for output. Terminals could either be hardwired to the computer or connected to them through a modem. The Teletype (TTY) Model 33 terminal (shown on the right) was slow, noisy, and produced medium quality output. It could output up to 10 characters per second. It used a narrower version of the printer paper used by the big line printers – that is, punched holes on the sides.

The daisywheel printer produced a big improvement in speed and print quality.

Figure 16: Daisywheel Print Head

It used a spinning head like the one shown above. If you wanted a different font, you simply removed the head that was on the printer and replaced it with another one. It had typewriter quality output.

Occasionally the circuit that synchronized when the hammer hit the character at the tip would fail and petals would go flying in the air!

Computers need hardware (and software) to enable them to talk to each other and peripheral devices. Mainframe computers and Minicomputers use different types of connections. In mainframes the data is sent as a block, replacing what was on the screen before.

Minicomputers used a standard called RS-232. It used a serial transmission approach (sending data one bit at a time). Over the years the speed improved, from 300 baud (bits per second) to 1,200 baud, to 2,400 baud, and finally to 9,600 baud. And there it stands.

If the terminal or printer is near the computer, a data cable is used to connect the two. If a terminal is not near the computer, it can be connected to it with a modem. A modem (modulator – demodulator) converts a signal from analog to digital or from digital to analog. You put one at the sending end and connect it to a telephone line. You put another at the receiving end and connect it to a telephone line. The data is converted to analog, sent across the telephone network to the other end where that modem converts it back to digital.

The Safeguard Anti-Missile system had a special device called the Data Transmission Controller (DTC) to communicate with other Safeguard Systems. I'd tell you how it works, but then I'd have to kill you.

What makes a computer fast / slow
With all the transistors that make up the CPU, it takes time for the electrons to make their way through the circuitry. Therefore

each computer has a "clock", a device that produces digital pulses. These pulses tell the CPU that the circuits are ready.

As an example, let's suppose we are in Biology class and the teacher has just announced the teams for the next lab project – dissecting a frog. She tells us to move so that the members of each team are sitting together. Some students move fast, others, not so fast. One student may not be able to sit down until the other had moved from that seat. Everybody is NOT immediately ready. But, if the teacher says, "It is 2:00 o'clock. In two minutes we will begin," everybody should have settled down.

As we are able to put more transistors on a chip, the time takes for the circuit to settle down is less and we can put in a faster clock. This makes the computer run faster.

The Intel 8080 uses a 2 megahertz clock. This meant that it pulses 2 million times a second (Note: Some operations take more than one clock cycle).

Another factor that effects the speed of a computer is the word length. The 8080 is an 8 bit processor. This means that it works with one byte at a time. To move 2 bytes takes two instructions. In contrast a 32 bit computer can move 4 bytes at a time. The 8 bit processor can only add a number up to 128. To add bigger number requires more steps. A 16 bit processor can add numbers up to 32,767, and a 32 bit one over 2 billion.

The IBM/360 Model 91 of 1964 could process up to 16 million instructions per second.

Faster memory also makes a computer run faster. However, even fast memory is much slower than the speed of the CPU. Why not build some very fast memory into the CPU? It would not be as large as RAM, but would help when we are executing a small set of instructions or accessing a small section of data. That is "cache memory."

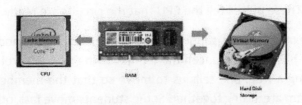

Figure 17: Cache and Virtual Memory

Here's an analogy: I am working at my desk, entering grades for my class. I have a big manual containing all the procedures to do this. They are in different sections of the manual. It takes time to find all the steps, searching through the manual. Instead I have written them down on a 3X5 card. With these few instructions I can quickly do the job.

We cannot build all our memory into the CPU, but we can put enough so that many operations that it does, use instructions / data from the cache. Now we have three levels of memory, cache which is very fast but limited in size, RAM which is slower but less costly, and our hard disk which has a lot of space but is very slow (compared to the CPU and RAM).

Another thing that slowed down the early computers was the fact that they had to wait for the input/output operations to complete. Any input/output device is extreeemly slow compared to the speed of the CPU. Why not add more hardware, an Input/Output Controller. Have the processor let this hardware transfer the data to/from the device and let the CPU know when it is done. When the CPU receives this "interrupt", it can stop what it is doing and handle the interrupt. It might send more data to the device and continue running the job.

This is one reason why you don't just hit the Power switch when you are done working. Sometimes the computer is still writing data from its buffers (areas in memory) to the output device(s). If you shut off the computer, data may be lost or corrupted.

Interrupt handling hardware and real-time clock hardware even lets the CPU switch running jobs periodically to give users their share of the computers resources' (Time Sharing). The computer switches between users so fast that each one thinks he / she has exclusive use of the computer.

3: A simple computer - CARDIAC / VISIAC

Now let's talk about a very simple computer, the CARDIAC. The acronym CARDIAC stands for "CARDboard Illustrative Aid to Computation." It was developed by David Hagelbarger at Bell Labs as a tool for teaching how computers work in a time when access to real computers was extremely limited. The CARDIAC kit consists of a folded cardboard "computer" and an instruction manual. In July 1969, the Bell Laboratories Record contained an article describing the system and the materials being made available to teachers for working with it.

The CARDIAC computer consisted of a left-hand CPU section and a right-hand memory section. On the CPU side there are five sliders:

- One slider of input "cards"
- One slider for the accumulator sign
- Three sliders for the digits of an instruction

The memory side has a single slider of output "cards." Portions of the sliders show through cutouts in the card frame. The cutouts for the input and output card sliders each show the current card to be read or written. The combination of the accumulator sign and the three instruction sliders show steps through cutouts that describe the operation of the selected instruction. Effectively, the sliders and cutouts are the instruction decoder of the CPU. Finally, each memory location has a hole in it. A small cardboard ladybug serves as the program counter which is moved from location to location in response to the steps described on the CPU side.

The VISIAC is a computer emulation[3] of the CARDIAC. Since it works exactly like the CARDIAC (except being an emulator made of computer instructions instead of cardboard), I will use it for all my explanations of simple computer operations from now on. Here's an analogy. When teaching a youngster to read would you give him / her a copy of War and Peace? Of course not. Why then would you tackle the operation of then Spectra 70 Mainframe Computer? No! Start with something simple.

VISIAC has an instruction set of 10 instructions and a memory of 100 cells. It does not have a multiply or divide instruction. You have to do these in programming (multiplication is repeated addition).

Let's compare it against the Altair 8800, the first home computer kit that a hobbyist could buy.

	VISIAC	Altair 8800
Speed	240 instructions per second	Few hundred thousand instructions per second
Number of Instructions	10	57
Memory	100 cells	4,000 bytes
Registers	3	9
Input	Card reader (emulated)	Toggle switches

---

[3] A computer program that makes a high-speed computer act like a different one.

Output	Card punch (emulated)	Lights

Figure 18: The Altair 8800

The VISIAC is only intended to be an instructional aid. Let's summarize what it can and cannot do:

What it can do:
Teach you the fundamentals of computer design
Teach you the fundamentals of programming

What it cannot do:
Show you how binary works
Support high-level languages (even BASIC)
Run complicated programs

4: The Home Computer

If we consider the 60's to be the era of the Mainframes, maybe we could consider the 70's and early 80's to be the era of the home computer. While the mainframes continued to evolve, a new type of computer is arising, the "Home Computer." As an example let's take the Apple IIE and the Commodore-64. Each had been preceded by earlier models. The C-64 had 64 thousand bytes of memory and supported 5 ¼" floppy disk drives (extra cost). Shortly after, it was replaced by the C-128. It had twice the memory and a processor with double the speed, I was amazed.

Figure 19: Apple IIE and Commodore 64

It worked primarily with text, but, like the C-64, had some simple graphics (to play simple games). It came with built-in BASIC and you could get a "C" compiler as well as word processing and spreadsheet programs (text only).

5: Operating Systems and System software

The original computers had no Operating Systems. The programmer loaded the code into the computer's memory (by using switches and lights) and ran it. He/she had to write all the code, including the complicated and tedious steps to read computer cards and print to the printer, in binary. If the program didn't work right, he/she had to fix the program and repeat the process. After the program finished, he/she could run it again or repeat the whole process to run a new program.

Then, somebody got a great idea, "Suppose we could write a program to run other programs. It could include all the code to do the input and output and save data to the storage devices so that the programmer could just tell this program to do them. Thus the Operating System was born.

The first Operating Systems were Single-Task ones. They would run one job, When it was finished they would run the next one.

They were NOT efficient for business use (remember, there were no computers for private use, unless you were John D. Rockefeller). If a job needed tape: BS-1278, the job would wait until the operator found that tape and loaded it (he/she might still be on a coffee break). The computer was just sitting there doing nothing until the tape was ready. Then developers came up with an operating system that got around that problem. It would put that job on hold and start running another one. If that one couldn't finish because it needed a resource, a third one would be started. This was the multi-tasking Operating System. Remember, throughput was the key! Have the computer do as much processing that it could. "User Friendliness" was not a priority. Trained operators ran these computers.

Is some situations, another factor was necessary. There was a system developed in the late 60's called "Safeguard." It was a military system designed to detect enemy missiles and fire our missiles to intercept them. It had to run in real-time. If necessary a low priority job would be pre-empted to run an important one (like the one that fired the missile). It also had special multi-processor hardware to make processing faster!

Types of Operating Systems

- Single-Task Operating Systems
- Multi-Task Operating Systems
- Real-Time Operating Systems

Operating Systems perform a number of functions:

- Controlling the running of application software
- Memory Management
    - Keeps track of memory locations to prevent programs and data from overlapping each other
    - Swaps portions of programs and data into the same memory but at different times
    - Keeps track of virtual memory

- Manages the File System
- Controls access to the files, folders and programs
- Provides a way for the users can communicate with the programs

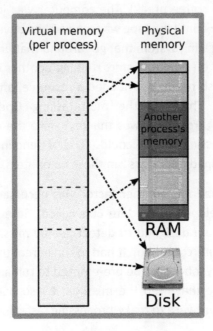

Figure 20: Virtual Memory

Virtual Memory deserves a little description. Having an executing program (or a set of programs) limited by the amount of physical memory is not desirable. What do we do (besides buying more memory)?

Let's start with VISIAC. VISIAC only has 100 cells of memory. Suppose our program was bigger. VISIOS[4] loads whatever part of the program fits in memory and starts running it. If the program calls for something that is not in the physical memory, VISIOS swaps out some of the program that is not being used to an

---

[4] VISIOS is VISIAC's Operating System - currently a piece of Vaporware (a piece of software that doesn't exist).

external device and uses that memory for the parts of the program that it needs. Later if it needs the parts that it swapped out, it will have to swap them back in. Now the program(s) are only limited by the storage of the external device.

In real computers the external device would be the hard disk. If the O/S only has to do this occasionally, no problem. But, if it has to do extensive swapping, the system may be very slow. This may occur if (besides the O/S which requires memory) you are running a lot of applications.

What's Inside an O/S – a simple description

I am going to describe what might be inside an operating system like UNIX. By using these words, I will hopefully keep a UNIX operating system expert from telling me what I said wrong.

An O/S serves as an interface between the application program and the computer hardware. An application program can have its own "virtual memory", but it certainly should not be able to look at or change another program's data. An application program should not be able to do anything that affects the integrity of the file system. The O/S controls these. It does this by providing a mechanism called "System Calls." If the program wants to create or delete a folder, it does a System Call. If it wants to read from a file, write to a file, create a file, or remove a file (directories are files), it does a System Call.

There's more. Sometimes a program wants to run another program. It may want to keep processing or wait until the other one finishes. UNIX has two system calls for this: "fork" and "exec." Fork tells the O/S to make a clone. Now there are two programs (we use the term processes) running, one designated as the parent, and the other as the child. The program can do a system call to find out which one it is. The child can issue an "exec" system call to have itself replaced by another program.

The parent can continue to do something else or go to sleep, waiting for the "death of a child" signal.

UNIX itself uses this approach to get itself started. The start program looks in a file that tells it what programs to start. They would typically be: programs to control the printer, programs to look for user to login, programs to communicate with other systems, and more. It uses the "fork/exec" mechanism to do this.

6: Application Software

The computers of this time need programs to do something useful. These are application programs. Usually they are written to perform scientific and business functions (like payroll calculations). Often they are written for a company's specific purposes and require a large staff of developers to create and maintain them. COBOL, PL/1 and FORTRAN were the common languages used (FORTRAN is still in use today).

7: Databases

In the late 60's IBM provided its Information Management System (IMS) database for use in the Apollo space program. It used a hierarchical model and was available only for Mainframe computers. IMS was used for large applications such as keeping records for all the plug-in equipment of a telephone company. These databases also required a large staff to develop and maintain them.

Section 2: The Future (The 90's)

June 1995						
Monday	Tuesday	Wednesday	Thursday	Friday	Saturday	Sunday
			1	2	3	4
5	6	7	8	9	10	11
12	13	14	15	16	17	18
19	20	21	22	23	24	25
26	27	28	29	30		

Now we are in the year 1995, twenty years into the future. In studying the evolution of dinosaurs, we talk about dozens of millions of years to see evolutionary trends (the development of new species and the extermination of others). In computers, these trends happen in dozens of years or less. Mainframes and servers have continued the evolutionary process. Speed has increased and size and cost has gone down.

8: Getting personal - the PC

Back in the 70's the Home Computer was emerging as an affordable device. Then in 1981 IBM introduced the PC. It was a little pricey compared to the home computers. But it was more suited to business applications such as word processing and spreadsheets. It originally came with a 13" screen with green or white text. Then they added a screen with 16 colors, WOW! The original pair of 5 ¼ inch floppy drives were later complimented by a 10 MB hard drive. It used the MS DOS operating system.

In the next 10 years the PC evolved remarkably. As a new model came out every few years all aspects of its performance improved.

Section 2: The Future (The 90's)

PC Processors

PROCESSOR	DATE INTRODUCED	NUMBER OF TRANSISTORS	WORD SIZE	TYPICAL CLOCK SPEED
8088	1979	29,000	16 bit	4.77 MHZ
80286	1982	134,000	16 bit	12
80386	1985	275,000	32 bit	16
Pentium	1993	1,200,000	64 bit	60
Pentium Pro	1995	5.5 million	64 bit	180

Figure 21: INTEL PC processors

The video card (the PC circuit board that produces the image on the monitor) has evolved in spurts as well as continuous evolution. The CGA (Computer Graphics Adapter) and EGA (Extended Graphics Adapter) cards gave way to the modern VGA (Video Graphics Array) card. The first VGA cards could produce a 640 X 480 pixel image. That meant 640 pixels across and 480 pixels down. The more color a pixel could have, the more video card memory was required. If you wanted 24 bit color, that meant almost a million bytes of memory. Now 1,600 X 900 or better with 24 bit color is common. Video now uses a graphics processing unit (GPU), a specialized processor used to manipulate three-dimensional (3-D) computer graphics.

Section 2: The Future (The 90's)

In addition Display cards on some PC's and almost all laptops support a second monitor. This means that you can show one item (like a Word document) on one screen and another item (like a web page) on the second screen. With a desktop you can show a third item by purchasing another video card and monitor. You are only limited by the number of card slots on your motherboard and the space on your desk to hold monitors.

With so many people having these computers at home, protecting them is important. A surge protector will keep a nearby lightning bolt from frying your motherboard. But when the power goes off you may lose whatever you were working on. The UPS (Uninterruptable Power Supply) comes to the rescue. It plugs into your electrical outlet and your devices plug into it. It contains batteries and if power is lost, it keeps your device running until the battery runs out. In the Data Center world large UPS's can keep their devices running for a period of time. Critical environments like hospitals have emergency backup generators that will kick in long before the UPS's run out. Note that battery powered devices like laptops do not have this problem.

9: Input / Output

The normal input devices, keyboard and mouse haven't changed too much. Wireless technology have freed us from having to be less than a few feet away from the computer (at the cost of having to replace batteries as needed).

Here's a question: When was the computer mouse invented? Answer:

1964

Monitors have changed in several ways. The original PC monitor size of 13" (first monochrome, then 16 color) has increased over the years. At first a bigger size would be costly, then become reasonably priced and the next larger size after that be costly. Now a 19" CRT cost no more than a 15" one of not that many years ago. Video cards evolved to match the monitors. With a resolution of 640 X 480 pixels and many colors, they now support graphics, not merely text.

Sound has changed over the years, PC's come with a small speaker. Its purpose is to tell you if something is drastically wrong with it. After all, if the video card is bad, how is the computer supposed to display an error message? The answer is "beeps." A set of long and short beeps tell the user what the problem is. You can look up the codes on the internet.

But to hear "real" sound and music you need a sound card and speakers. Both have improved; the more you pay, the better quality you get.

10: Portable Computers

In 1982 Compaq introduced a portable computer. Now for the first time you could take a computer with you.

While they were definitely portable, they were questionably laptops. But then real laptops came out. As in any new device, they were pricy and were nowhere near as powerful as a desktop computer. They didn't even have color screens.

Section 2: The Future (The 90's)

But as the desktops improved, so did the laptops. While they were always a bit more expensive and not as powerful, they were a good alternative for people who traveled.

11: Mobile Devices

There is a device that is so common that almost every strip mall has a store selling or renting them. I'm talking about the pager, a small handheld device that enables you to tell who is trying to call you.

Another mobile device that is just a little expensive for personal use, but highly desirable for business use is the Portable Data Assistant (PDA). The Palm Pilot was a highly successful one.

Section 2: The Future (The 90's)

Let's talk about another mobile device. I am now going to talk to man on the street. "Sir, I see some gadget in your hand. What is it?"

"It's a cell phone. With it I can make calls from anywhere in the United States. Well perhaps not anywhere. When I get out of the country I lose the signal."

"Sir, could you imagine that in about ten or fifteen years your cell phone could take and show pictures, play music, and play games?"

"What kind of weed do you think I'm smoking?"

12: Fun and games

The idea of playing games on a computer has not quite been around since the beginning. ENIAC was designed to calculate ballistic trajectories and the commercial computers designed shortly after that were only concerned with business operations. But even the PDP computer of the mid 70's had a text based adventure game. The Atari home computer of the 80's introduced a whole series of games to the home audience. One of my favorite computers, the commodore-64, had an extensive set of games. Add a joystick and you could be entertained for hours.

With Microsoft Windows came Solitaire, in my mind the most executed application in its repertoire. With faster hardware, including enhanced graphics cards, computer games got better. Besides the action games, PC's also added board games. By now, I would guess that few home players can beat a good chess program. And it has been over 10 years since a computer beat the best chess player (and since then computers have become much more powerful).

Section 2: The Future (The 90's)

In 2016 a computer will beat a top ranked professional Go player (I consider Go to be a harder game than chess).

Now we have a number of game computers, special purpose computers designed specifically to play games. They have powerful processors and graphics cards, and a mind boggling assortment of games. While computer input devices have not changed too much through the years, game computer ones have. Joysticks have been supplemented by wireless hand held controllers, steering wheels, drums and guitars (within a decade even your body movements will control your game).

Even the cell phone arena has been infected with games like Tetras and Snake. The future will see Smartphones with games like Scrabble, FreeCell (my favorite) and Sudoku They will keep the user occupied for hours. Add to that, action games, and the Smartphone or iPad is almost a play station in itself.

13: Operating Systems

In the 70's and earlier, computers were either supercomputers, mainframes, or minicomputers. They were used for business purposes, scientific work, or military use. Now with the infestation of the PC we need a different kind of Operating System. Considering the size and power of the PC compared to these big computers, we had to start over. Besides not being able to run those Mainframe / Minicomputer Operating Systems because of the PC's limited capacity and processing speed, we had another consideration: "User Friendliness."

In 1985 Microsoft introduced a "Windows" Operating System. Until then, the PC used DOS, a "Command Line" based system. That meant that the user typed a command on the screen and the result was sent as text to the screen.

Section 2: The Future (The 90's)

```
C:\Users\Marc>dir
 Volume in drive C is Windows8-HP
 Volume Serial Number is EA62-748E

 Directory of C:\Users\Marc

11/18/2017  02:04 PM    <DIR>          .
11/18/2017  02:04 PM    <DIR>          ..
03/13/2017  06:49 AM    <DIR>          .android
01/31/2015  10:55 AM    <DIR>          .AndroidStudio
11/11/2015  08:47 AM    <DIR>          .AndroidStudio1.4
03/13/2017  06:48 AM    <DIR>          .AndroidStudio2.3
08/19/2016  06:01 PM    <DIR>          .dnx
10/08/2016  01:08 AM    <DIR>          .fontconfig
03/05/2017  12:15 PM    <DIR>          .gimp-2.6
12/03/2017  06:46 AM    <DIR>          .gimp-2.8
11/14/2015  09:16 AM    <DIR>          .gradle
04/04/2017  09:06 AM    <DIR>          .kindle
04/04/2017  10:36 AM    <DIR>          .oracle_jre_usage
10/08/2016  01:11 AM    <DIR>          .thumbnails
```

Figure 22: Command Line Interface

When the PC finished running one program, the user could then enter another command.

With Windows, the computer became vastly more user friendly. Now that the graphics card could produce pixels instead of just characters, a Graphical User Interface (GUI) could be employed. The PC could display pictures, not just text. In addition, a mouse (a pointing device) could be used to select an object on the screen.

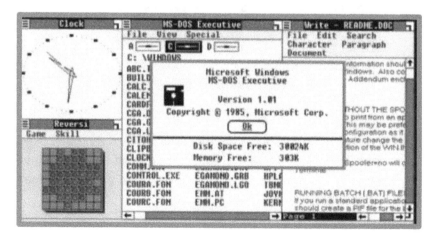

Section 2: The Future (The 90's)

Another problem with MS/DOS was that it couldn't run a program that was larger than the available memory. Your only choice was to buy more memory or not run the program.

The solution was to use Virtual Storage, a concept already used by the large mainframe computers. Multiple Virtual Storage (MVS) was an Operating System used on the IBM System/370 computers. If the computer needed more memory for a job, it swapped some memory contents to the hard disk. When it needed it again, it would swap it back. This would slow the computer down, but it could run jobs that required more memory than the computer actually had.

The Boot Process

How do we get the O/S running? In the early days of computers the user / operator had to load a program into the computer by hand (setting switches on and off) to get the computer started. A slight improvement was to load the program from some media. A computer I was introduced to in my college days used a paper tape with holes in it. A reader would load a simple program from the tape. This was called booting. By the time we got to home computers and PC's the process got a lot simpler.

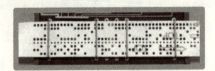

Figure 24: Punched Paper Tape

The term refers to boots and the straps that some boots have attached to help the wearer pull them on and to the imagined feat of a lifting oneself off the ground by pulling on one's bootstraps.

Section 2: The Future (The 90's)

Booting starts when we turn on the computer. It uses special memory instructions inside the computer, the BIOS. The BIOS (Basic Input / Output System) contains the instructions needed to get us started. It is contained in a special type of memory called ROM[5] (Read Only Memory) Unlike RAM, ROM keeps its values when the computer is turned off.

The BIOS has instructions to first check to see if the computer has basic sanity (that's why if you lean on the keyboard while it is checking, it reports an error). If it detects an error after it knows that it has enough sanity, it puts the message on the screen. If it doesn't even have enough sanity to do so, it beeps.

Once its hardware test is completed, it is ready to load the O/S, but from where? A setting that you can change tells it what device to look at first to load the O/S from. The default device is the first (or only) hard disk drive. There is a sector of data on the device called the "boot block" that tells the BIOS where to load the O/S from. If there is no "boot block" on the device it tries the next device on its list. Booting from another device may be desired (or required if you have to boot from it to fix or restore your O/S).

Once it has found a valid "boot block" it loads the O/S and starts running it.

Sophisticated users can set up a "multi-boot" system. If the "boot block" points to a small program with a menu of available O/S's, it runs it. The user can then select the one they want and it is loaded and run. GRUB is an example of a menu program.

---

[5] ROM can be changed using special procedures.

Section 2: The Future (The 90's)

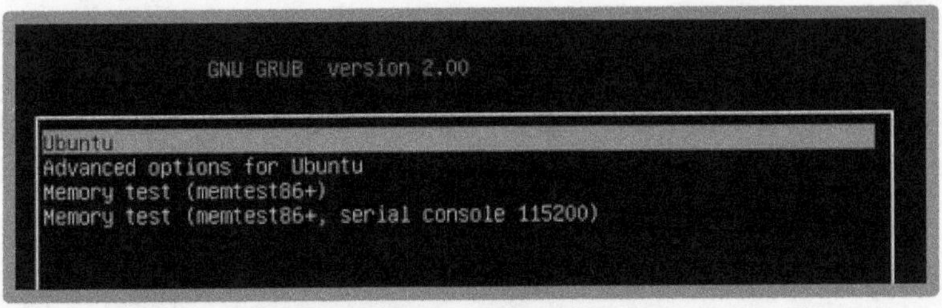

Figure 25: The GRUB Boot Loader

PC operating systems use a hierarchical (in simple terms, a tree structure) structure for storing files and folders. First we have to define some terms. Microsoft uses a "\" as the separator between folders, UNIX/Linux and MAC OS use a "/." Microsoft uses a letter ("C","D", ...) for naming the device (the first hard drive, the second hard drive, the CD drive, etc.). The letters "A", and "B" are reserved for floppy disk drives (soon to become extinct). UNIX/Linux use a method called "mounting" (beyond the scope of this book). The terms "folder" and "directory" are the same. Microsoft also uses the concept of file suffixes. After the file name is a period followed by (usually) three letters. They identify the type of file. For example a ".doc" or a ".docx" file is a Microsoft Word file. A ".exe" file is an executable program. Even though some programs don't care what the suffix is, many do, and it is NOT a good idea for you to change the suffix. Microsoft and MAC OS are NOT case sensitive, "hello.txt" and "HELLO.TXT" refer to the same file. UNIX/Linux are case sensitive (note that passwords are almost always case sensitive). UNIX/Linux files have permissions for reading, writing, or executing a file. There are permissions for the owner of the file, his/her group, or for anyone. Thus, you can make a file writable by only the owner, readable only by the owner's group of users, and executable by everybody.

Section 2: The Future (The 90's)

At the bottom is the root folder ("\" for Microsoft or "/" for UNIX/Linux and MAC OS). The root folder can contain files or other folders. Each of these folders can contain files or other folders. A file can contain text, a picture, music, a program, or other types of data. The user can make this structure as complicated as required. Below is a simplified example of what might be in a Microsoft "C:" drive:

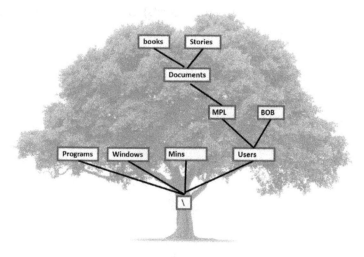

Figure 26: Sample File Structure

More System Software

Another piece of system software is the DLL (Dynamic Link Library). If you've run application programs on a PC that opens or save files, you've noticed that the dialog box looks the same. It is the same code. In the old days each program would have that code built into it. Now the code is in a library file called a DLL. When you run the program it dynamically loads the DLL(s) it needs into memory to give the program the code it needs. If a

DLL is missing, the program won't run properly. Setup programs for applications make sure that the needed DLL's are available (also when you remove a program properly, the unneeded DLLs are also removed).

O/S's usually come with utilities to maintain the health of your O/S. One of those (for Windows) is Defrag. The Windows file system is composed of disk tracks and sectors. A disk may have one or more platters (like vinyl records). Data is written onto one or more sectors.

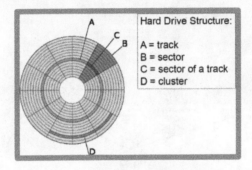

Figure 27: Hard Drive Structure

The bigger the file, the more sectors are required. If a file gets bigger and the next sector is not available, another sector on the disk is used. It may be on another track or even another platter. Just like with records if you have to go to another place on the disk, it takes more time. If your disk has a lot of free space, you don't have a problem. If you don't have a lot of free space, your disk may be fragmented and the O/S will take more time loading or saving the data.

The situation is like what happens if you write a list of your friends' names and their phone numbers on a piece of paper. You organize them nicely, in alphabetical order. Then you add more. Pretty soon the page starts to get loaded. You put the new names on the bottom or in the margins, with arrows pointing to their proper location. After a while it is pretty bad and you decide to make a new list. Now you can get at your information easily.

Defrag helps when your disk is fragmented. It moves the data around so that the file information is on adjacent sectors. Depending on the size of your hard disk and the amount of free space, it may take a lot of time.

Of course, it does not remove any files. There may be a lot of files on the disk that you don't want. Sometimes temporary files do not get removed. There are utilities (like "SimCleaner") that do this. It is a good idea to run them periodically.

Virus checkers and Firewalls are especially valuable if your computer is hard-wired to the Internet. Seriously, do NOT ignore them!

Backup and Recovery tools are also part of System Utilities. Do NOT ignore them either! Many people decide to do backups shortly after critical information has been lost (another example of Murphy's Law).

14: Application Software

Application software, the programs that perform useful functions for the user are important tools for all users. There are literally many thousands of application programs. They span the platforms from PC's and Mac's to UNIX and mainframes.

Since we can't cover them all here, let's try to put them into categories.

- Business
- Finance
- Personal software
- Entertainment

Section 2: The Future (The 90's)

- Audio, video and pictures

Suites for the Sweet

Business software includes word processors, spreadsheets, presentation software, project management software, and database software.

What was the first spreadsheet developed for a personal computer? Answer:

VisiCalc

Often the company that developed these applications will bundle them up into a package called a "suite." Buying the suite is less expensive than buying the applications individually and the have some common features. Microsoft Office, LibreOffice and Open Office are some examples.

They all provide common basic functionality. A document created in one word processor can be edited in the other. The look and feel may be slightly different, but the user can easily get used to the differences. Should we look at them as identical twins or fraternal twins? I think the latter. If you go too far beyond the basic features you see some incompatibilities. Master documents created in Microsoft Word and those created in LibreOffice Writer are incompatible. Custom Slide Shows created in PowerPoint are invisible to LibreOffice Impress and vice-versa. There are other minor differences, but not enough to make me worry about which one I am using.

Word Makes a Difference

The one business application that is often of use in both a work environment and a home one is the word processor. The concepts and features are the same whether you use Microsoft Office, LibreOffice, or Open Office (or others). The look and feel may be slightly different among different products or even different versions, but you can easily accommodate yourself to the differences.

When I ask my class to rate their proficiency in a scale from 1 to 10 (where 9 or 10 means that they are proficient with most of its features and 1 means that the might not recognize it if they fell over it), there are a few 1's and 2's, 9's, and 10's with most people in the middle.

Most of the time, the user is typing text and editing it. The only slight difference is that the Office Clipboard allows you to copy up to 24 items from Office documents or other programs and paste them into another Office document.

A wonderful feature, but one you have to be careful about is the spelling and grammar checker.

Hear is on example of why you should nut trust spellcheck!

Documents can be saved in many formats. You can even create PDF documents and web pages as well as plain text files (if you do that, all formatting will be lost).

How often to save your file is a matter of personal preference. If someone asks me, I ask them: "What is your level of pain if your changes get lost?" The higher your level of pain, the more often you should save your file. If you are just making simple additions or corrections, save it to the same place. If you are trying some exotic changes, you may want to save the file under a different name (e.g. "Book Formatting Test.docx"). That way if you really screw something up you can go back to the original.

How fancy do you want to get?

Sometimes we need a sophisticated program; sometimes just a simple one. Here's an example. Suppose we just want to make a shopping list, a to-do list, or some notes. Almost anything will do.

Section 2: The Future (The 90's)

We don't need pictures, colors or different fonts or font sizes. In this case a simple text editor or an app like Color Notes will do fine. But, if we are doing something more sophisticated (like writing this book) a good Word Processor is required. Even a simple Word Processor like WordPad won't cut it (it doesn't even have a Spelling Checker or a Grammar Checker). There are a number of choices, some that you pay for, and others that are freeware. You can even get some that run on tablets and Smartphones, although I wouldn't suggest writing a novel on one.

Spinning my web [Site]

Most of my readers who are competent in surfing the web would be at a loss to design their own web site. Whereas I would in no way consider that I have the skills and talent to create a web site for a large retailer, I can and have created sites for small businesses and organizations. The hard part is the "look and feel" of the site and the material – text and pictures – that should go in it.

```
1
2  <html>
3
4  <head>
5  <meta http-equiv="Content-Type" content="text/html; charset=windows-1252">
6  <meta http-equiv="Content-Language" content="en-us">
7  <meta name="GENERATOR" content="Microsoft FrontPage 4.0">
8  <meta name="keywords" content="lighthouses,museums.barnegat light">
9  <meta name="ProgId" content="FrontPage.Editor.Document">
10
11
12 <title>Home</title>
13 <meta name="Microsoft Border" content="t">
14 </head>
15
16 <body background="_themes/ricepapr/ricebk.jpg"  ><!--msnavigation--><table border="0" cel
17
18 <p align="center"><br>
19 <font size="5"><b>
20 <nobr>[ Home ]</nobr> <nobr>[ <a href="about_the_museum.htm">About The Museum</a> ]</nobr
21 <p align="center"><b><font size="6" color="#000080">Barnegat Light Historical
22 Society and Museum</font></b></p>
23
24 </td></tr><!--msnavigation--></table><!--msnavigation--><table border="0" cellpadding="0"
25
```

Figure 28: Example of HTML

Section 2: The Future (The 90's)

Similarly to the way that software development evolved, web site development evolved. Developing programs by writing in machine language was nasty. Creating web pages in HTML was not much better. Developers would use a text editor to create the web page, then check it out, using a browser (probably a few browsers). The web site rental itself was not cheap.

Now there are more and more tools (like Microsoft's "Front Page") that let you create web sites without knowing HTML. The tool lets you create a web page similarly to the way you would create a page using a word processor. It translates what you wrote into HTML and provides tools to upload the page to your web site (I expect "Front Page" will be retired and replaced by fancier tools – some on the Internet itself.

If your only tool is a hammer, everything looks like a nail
Microsoft Word was the favorite tool of a person I knew. He would write his research papers with it (good), his to-do lists (OK) and his web pages (wrong tool). There are software tools for almost every purpose. If you are only doing some function occasionally, you may want to use the tool that you are familiar with. But, if you are doing some function frequently (or are having somebody else maintain it) I recommend using the proper tool. There may be a number of tools that work, so you have to pick one.

I personally have occasionally used a tool when a better one was available. Some of the figures in this book that contain text, pictures and arrows were done in PowerPoint. A better tool would have been LibreOffice Draw. It could have been worse. Gimp has the ability to create pictures with layers. I could have put each object (picture, textbox, arrows) on a separate layer. It would work, but would be very difficult to maintain.

Where do you get software from?

There are a number of ways to obtain software:

- Buy it in stores or on the web.
- Download or copy Public Domain software. You can use it or modify it without any fee.
- Download Freeware. Freeware is copyrighted software that is distributed free of charge.
- Download Shareware. You get to use it for a trial period or a specified number of uses. If you want to use it after that, you have to pay for it.
- Run software on the web.
- Sign up for Rentalware. Rentalware is online software that users lease for a fee and download it whenever they want it.
- Make it yourself or have a developer custom make a software package.

Unless you are using a PC or laptop, your software will probably be downloaded from the web.

15: Databases come of age

Databases, which were in the realm of Mainframes and Minicomputers up until now, have come to PC's. Relational Databases are starting to replace the older Hierarchal Databases in Mainframes and are now available under Windows. They have the same type of features that the ones on larger computers have, but their speed and processing power is less.

Databases are such an important tool for business that they deserve their own section. A Database is an organized collection of data. A Relational Database (the type most used in the modern business world) consists of one or more tables of data. If a record in the table is a "key field", records in other tables can be joined to that record. Here is an example of real database table. Note that the user can sort by any column simply by clicking on the "▼" at the top of the column. This works whether there are a hundred rows or a hundred thousand rows (it might take longer).

Object Nbr ▾	Object ▾	Description ▾	Category ▾	Donor ▾	Date Receive ▾	Location ▾	On Loan
1	Soap dish from	White with green patt	Plates / Silverw:	Bertha Axelson		South Wall	☐
3	Lens plate	Descriptive plate			5/1/1956		☐
5	Blue Willow din	Oceanic or Social Hote	Plates / Silverw:			South Wall	☐
6	Lighthouse keep	White plate/brown bo	Plates / Silverw:			South Wall	☐
7	Plate	Bordered plate	Plates / Silverw:			South Wall	☐
8	Cup and Saucer	Last cup and saucer fr	Plates / Silverw:	Mr. & Mrs. C. G		South Wall	☐
9	Navy Dept. Chin		Plates / Silverw:	Mrs. O'Hare		South Wall	☐
10	cup	Demitasse cup/Tepco	Plates / Silverw:			South Wall	☐
13	Goblet	Large glass	Plates / Silverw:			South Wall	☐
14	Napoleon cup &		Plates / Silverw:	Mr and Mrs. C. I		South Wall	☐
16	Pedestal dish	White compote with p	Plates / Silverw:			South Wall	☐
17	Wine bottle	Green glass	Plates / Silverw:			South Wall	☐

Figure 29: A Relational Database Table

Let's figure out why we need them. If you had something very simple (like a shopping list), any tool would do (notepad, a word document, a spreadsheet, or even writing it down on a piece of paper). If you have more items, a spreadsheet is more desirable. You can organize your data into worksheets and do simple sorting and searching. This will work fine for dozens or even hundreds of items. But suppose you have thousands or tens of thousands of items, or more. I don't think you want to use a spreadsheet. A database is an ideal tool for this.

Here's an example. Suppose you are going to start a new business, selling lighthouse gifts. They might include books, paintings, photographs, models, and more.

You have inventory. Each item should have a unique number identifying it. It needs a name, a description, cost and price information, how many new and used items you have (maybe how many "on-order"). This information would be in a table.

You have customers (hopefully). Each customer should have a unique number identifying him/her. He/she should have an address, one or more phone numbers, an E-Mail, and a few more fields.

You have orders. Each order should have a unique number identifying it. It should have the customer ID, the Item ID, and other information specific to the order. Note: you don't need the customer's address since you have the customer ID and that will point to the row in the customer table with that information. We now have related the information in one table to information in other tables – hence a Relational Database.

You may want to add another table, the list of Categories for the items. You wouldn't want to put one picture in the category "paintings", and another in the category "photos." The form that allows you to add or edit items would be programmed only to accept the list of valid categories.

A typical Database system includes:

- Tools to create and maintain tables
- Backup and Recovery tools
- Tools to create forms
- Tools to create Reports
- Support for Structured Query Language (SQL)

These tools and concepts apply whether the Database is a small one with hundreds of records to one with millions of records...

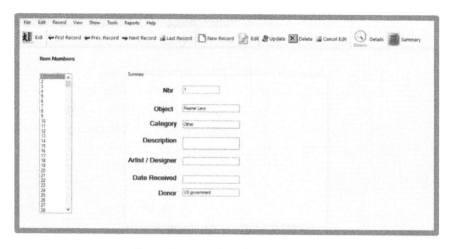

Figure 30: A Database form

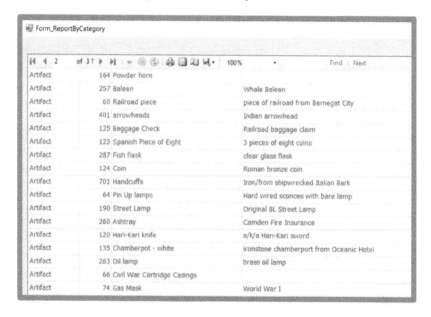

Figure 31: Database Report

Structured Query Language (SQL) is a very useful tool for working with Databases. Most Databases support this language: Here's an example:

Section 2: The Future (The 90's)

> SELECT CUSTOMER_NAME, CUSTOMER_E_MAIL FROM CUSTOMERS WHERE CUSTOMER_STATE = NY

This query would return the name and E-Mail from every customer record in the "CUSTOMERS" table where his/her state is "NY." It doesn't care whether there are a hundred records in the table or a hundred thousand records (of course it might take a little longer to do the processing).

Here's another:

> DELETE FROM CUSTOMERS WHERE CUSTOMER_LAST_ORDER_DATE < "12/1/2005"

I would need another book to completely describe the SQL language and how to use it.

16: The Software Development Process Gets Better

The process of the 70's was tedious. The developer first had to write the code (using terminals or punched cards) and then compile it and run it. The developer had to go back and forth between the editor, compiler and debugger programs (often MANY times) until the program worked properly. With the Integrated Development Environment (IDE) this all changed. The developer now runs one program (e.g. Visual Studio).

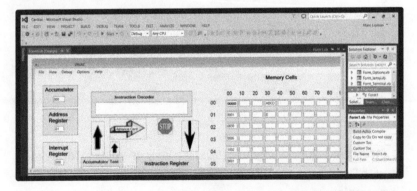

Section 2: The Future (The 90's)

Figure 32: A Visual Studio Form Development screen

Figure 33: A Visual Studio Code Development screen

Within this one program, the developer can create and modify the screens (forms), write and debug the code, and publish the finished product.

Section 3: The Far Future (The 2015's)

Let's go ahead another twenty years.

17: Moore's Law is still the law of the land

Computer hardware, including the CPU and memory continues to grow as predicted.

More Processors

PROCESSOR	DATE INTRODUCED	NUMBER OF TRANSISTORS	WORD LENGH	TYPICAL CLOCK SPEED
8088	1979	29,000	16 bit	4.77 MHz
80386	1985	275,000	32 bit	16 MHz
		...		
Pentium D	2005	230 million	64 bit dual core	2.66 GHz

Section 4: Then and Now

Xeon	2009	781 million	64 bit 10 core	2.4 GHz
AMD Bulldozer	2012	1.2 billion	64 bit 8 core	3.6 GHz
AMD Epyc	2017	19.2 billion	64 bit 32 core	2.2 GHz
Qualcom Snapdrago n 835	2016	3 billion	64 bit 8 core	2.35 GHz

Figure 34: More Processors[6]

We have had 64-bit CPU's and software that makes use of it for about ten years. But, what does that mean? 64-bit architecture means that the computer can work with eight bytes of data at a time as opposed to the four bytes at a time that 32-bit architecture can handle.

Figure 35: Laptop Motherboard

Does that mean that the computer runs twice as fast? Let's look at yet another analogy: Suppose you have to move your office furniture from one building to another. You get a van and make one trip. If you had used your minivan you would have had to

---

[6] These are just some examples.

Section 4: Then and Now

make two trips. But suppose all you had to move was your PC, printer, and copier. You could use your minivan and make one trip. Similarly if you are moving large amounts of data from memory area to another, 64-bit architecture will make the process run faster. To take advantage of this, you need a 64-bit O/S. If you have a 64-bit O/S, you can run 64-bit application software. Note that 32-bit OS's and software will run on a 64-bit processor.

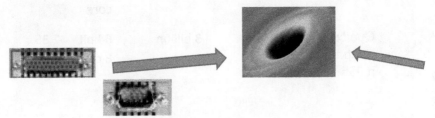

Figure 36: The Death of Parallel and Serial Ports

While PC's are still important, the laptop has replaced the desktop as a computer of choice for many people. In 1998 USB-1.1 became available. We're now up to USB-3. It is 10 times faster than USB 2.0 and 400 times faster than USB 1.1. Now a laptop could be connected to a number of devices, printers, scanners, CD player/recorders and more (USB hubs can be used when you have more USB devices than ports.

In the past, devices such as scanners needed a circuit card in the computer for connectivity. Maybe if I had a hammer and chisel, I could fit one in your laptop (just kidding).

For a long time clock speed was a measure of how powerful a CPU was, along with other factors such as whether it was a 32 bit processor or a 64 bit one. Then (remember Moore's Law) they were able to put more than one processor "core" in the CPU. They put 2, 4, 6, and then more "cores" on the CPU chip. Does this mean that a PC with a 4 core CPU runs four times faster than a 1 core one? If one chef can cook a turkey in four hours, can four chefs cook it in one hour? But, in situations when parts of a job can run simultaneously, it will run faster. This technology has even worked its way into Smartphones and tablets (note that the Qualcom processor listed above is used in many of today's Smartphones).

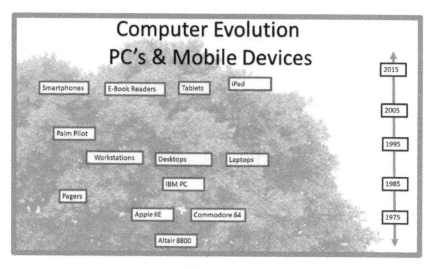

Figure 37: The PC (and Mobile Device) Tree

The Hard Drive Becomes Harder, Faster and More Reliable

From the time of the first hard drive for PC's, they have become faster, smaller, cheaper. They also provide much more storage. A hard drive of the 90's that was 5¼ inches wide and would hold about 500 megabytes has been replaced by a 3 ½ inch wide one that holds a few terabytes (gigabyte is a billion, terabyte is 1,000 billion). In the days when hard drive size first exceeded 540 megabytes, the EIDE (Extended Integrated Drive Electronics) still used the 40 pin ribbon cables for connectivity. Then the SATA interface replaced it. It was over four times faster and only

71

required a 7 pin connector. It was also a lot easier to attach multiple drives.

Portable hard drives using USB can now extend the storage capacity of your PC. The technology still used rotating disk(s) and a read head that moved to access the proper sector.

You can buy an adapter that lets you connect an IDE, EIDE or SATA drive to your USB connection on your PC or laptop. This can be used to test the drive or get data from/to it.

Figure 38: A Hard Drive Exposed

For situations where it is critical that a hard drive failure does not cause the system to go down, there is RAID (Redundant Array of Independent/ Inexpensive Disks). The simplest one uses mirroring. There are two disks with data being written to them simultaneously. If one fails, the data is still on the other. The system will still work, and later the bad drive can be replaced. However, you require twice as many disk drives. RAID V uses five disk drives to store four drives worth of data. The data is spread across all the disks, so if one fails, the data is still on the other ones.

In the 90's the CD and later the DVD were the only inexpensive ways to store small and medium amounts of data (4.7 GB for a single sided, single density DVD). Then solid state storage devices became available. The flash drive, using USB and its cousin the SD Card, were now a viable way to store data. At first they were small (their capacity less than 1 megabyte). But they grew quickly. Now a 32 Gigabyte one is common and inexpensive, and bigger ones are available. Many laptops and tablets have a slot for an SD or micro SD card.

Wait, there's more. Being solid state, these devices are faster and more reliable than hard disk drives which have mechanical parts. As their capacity grew and the price per gigabyte went way down, something wonderful happened. That technology became available for larger storage devices – the solid state drive. Although they are currently more expensive per gigabyte than a traditional one, they are getting cheaper.

The TV goes digital and becomes smart

The TV, which has been around since the 40's, was an analog device. The audio and video signals were analog. The audio was FM and not as subject to noise and interference as the video signal was. If you were far from the TV station, your picture quality often suffered (especially if your antenna was not aimed properly). Then in the late 90's TV went digital. The quality of the picture improved greatly. Due to the nature of digital signals, the picture was either there (with perfect quality) or not.

Section 4: Then and Now

An example of Murphy's Law was that if you were watching football using an HDTV antenna, the signal would get interrupted precisely when the most critical play of the game occurred.

TV's became "smart" in the 2010's. They are now special purpose computers, complete with apps. Even though I can't do word processing and E-Mail on my TV (not yet), I can attach a keyboard and mouse, as well as connect it to my laptop and my USB storage devices.

18: Special Purpose Computers

It's now hard to imagine how many everyday objects have special purpose computers in them. Suppose all the computers at your house stopped working! You can't make a cup of coffee. Your microwave oven won't microwave. Your TV won't work. Your house is cold because your WI-FI thermostat won't turn on the heat. So you decide to just give up and go to work. Forget it, your car won't start! At least, because I'm old fashioned, I don't have to worry about my refrigerator talking to my smartphone.

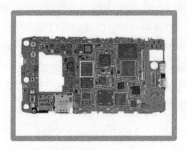

Figure 39: Smartphone Motherboard

Here's another special purpose computer, a hearing aid. Until the last few decades, a hearing aid was basically a microphone, an amplifier and a speaker. It got smaller (the early ones were the size of a deck of cards) through the years. Now they are computers with several microphones and sophisticated software. The more expensive models are ones with more sophisticated software. They can do things like reducing

74

background noise while boosting the volume of the person talking to you. They are now so small that they are often hard to notice. One of the models has the equivalent of an 11 core processor.

Drawing the Line

When I was a kid and a bully drew a line in the dirt and dared you to step across it, you knew that if you did so, you would get punched. This is a different kind of line. Let's go back to the 80's and talk about PC's and microcomputers. A PC was about $2,500 and sat on your desk. A Microcomputer was about $10,000 and sat in a large room. You certainly knew the difference between the two.

Now there is often a hazy line between categories. Is it a small Mainframe or a large Server? Is it a large PC or a small Workstation? When we talk about general purpose computers and special purpose computers, we often have ones that don't fit in one category or the other.

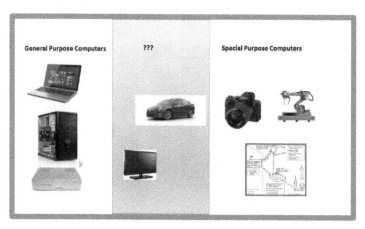

A Smart TV has apps. You can attach a mouse or keyboard to it. What is it? My car has apps and I can talk to it. What is it?

Section 4: Then and Now

19: Input / Output

Input devices have improved. The mouse, which used to have a ball inside, now has a laser. You don't have to periodically open it up and remove the lint. For those who have laptops and don't want to attach a mouse, the laptop includes some type of pointing device. The most common is a touchpad.

We have a new input device, the touch screen. We were starting to have a problem with devices such as a camcorder. It was hard to fit all those buttons on its side panel. Now, with the touch screen, we can have as many as we need. Similarly for the cell phone, we can not only have the buttons that we need, but also a keyboard.

Almost all laptops and portable devices come with cameras (sometimes two) and speakers. A device that was a science fiction staple of the past is now a reality – the Picture phone. With Skype and FaceTime – its Apple equivalent, you can have a videophone conversation with anyone in the world.

The technology has also extended to monitors. Many PC's and laptops come with touch screen monitors. A museum I am involved with has one to allow our visitors to view information about a topic just by pressing the appropriate spot on the screen.

Section 4: Then and Now

In the 90's bar code readers were a standard tool for business use. Now, when doing inventory, a store employee could simply scan the item instead of writing the information down on a clipboard. But they were not used for personal use. Today, with our smartphone with its built-in camera and access to the internet, we can scan a bar coded item at the supermarket to get its information.

Output devices have blossomed. Charles Darwin's Theory of Evolution as he envisioned it stated that there is a gradual evolution of creatures throughout time. Later it was determined that creatures change very little throughout large periods of time and then change drastically or become extinct. Such is the case with the CRT terminal. After gradually changing from a 13" monochrome screen to a 19" color one, it has now disappeared, being replaced by flat screen monitors and flat screen TV's. I was going to say that they have no use in today's world, but if one needs a paperweight or wants to exercise and doesn't have a set of weights, they may be useful.

To Print or Not to Print

In printers alone the user has numerous choices.

Types of printers
- Inkjet
- Mobile
- Laser
- Multifunction
- Photo Printer
- Plotter
- Dot Matrix Printer
- Thermal Printer
- Thermal Wax Printer
- 3D Printer
- Specialty Printers

Some are for general purpose printing, others for commercial or special purposes.

The most common printer type is the ink jet printer. It is inexpensive and produces letter quality output. It does this by shooting tiny jets of ink onto the paper. All modern ink jet printers support color. Some do this using a cartridge with four colors, magenta, cyan, and yellow, and another for black. Some have cartridges for the individual colors. Each has its advantages. If you are printing a lot of pages in one color, individual cartridges may be better. Otherwise a four color one may be better.

Sometimes it would be nice to be able to bring a printer with you. Whereas a laptop is easy to carry around, a normal ink jet printer isn't – thus the portable printer. They are small and easy to carry around. Some are battery powered.

A slightly more expensive version of the ink jet printer is the photo printer. It has inks that are less prone to fading and smearing. In addition it may have the ability to print from your camera or memory card without requiring a computer.

Multi-function printers combine the features of a scanner / copier / fax and printer. Since they are only slightly more expensive than ink jet printers alone, they are the preferred choice for many users. They range in features such as fax capability and multi-page scanning. Most modern ones support WI-FI and can be connected to your network (thus you don't have to connect it to a specific computer and have that computer on to use the printer). Multi-function laser printers are also available.

The family of laser jet printers cover those for personal and small business use to those for use in large companies. A laser jet printer is faster than an ink jet printer and more economical on supplies. Instead of ink cartridges, they use toner cartridges. Toner is a powdery substance that when heated inside the printer, fuses to the paper. Inexpensive ones only print in black and white and are slightly more expensive than ink jet printers. If

Section 4: Then and Now

you pay more money, you can get ones that print faster, ones that can print on both sides of the paper, and ones that print in color. Their color pictures are not as good as ink jet pictures.

Do NOT use ink jet photo paper in a laser printer! It will damage the printer!

Some modern creatures have been around from before the dinosaurs, like the alligator. One type of printer like that is the dot matrix printer. Its print head has tiny pins that punch through the ribbon to the paper.

The original ones had nine pins and produced low quality output. Later they came up with twenty-four pin printers. They could produce what they called "near-letter quality."

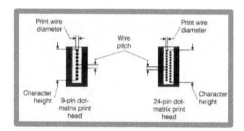

Figure 40: Dot matrix printer print heads

They still have a place today! Think about a tire repair shop. They need to print a receipt with a copy for the customer. They don't want to worry about replacing (expensive) print cartridges and don't care about a little extra noise. They don't want to take the time to print two copies like they would have to do with an ink jet or laser printer. A dot matrix printer is ideal.

Another type of special purpose printer used in the business world is the thermal printer. It uses special paper that turns dark when heat is applied to it. They don't even need ink. The paper is inexpensive and the print is low quality. After a while the print fades so that you have dark gray print on light gray paper. But, it

Section 4: Then and Now

is ideal for restaurants, libraries, and other places where quality is not important.

Typical Attributes of Printers						
Type of Printer	Cost of Printer	Cost of Media	Speed	Quality	Noisy	Size of Printer
Inkjet	-	-	-	-	-	-
Mobile	↑	-	-	-	-	↓
Laser	↑ to ↑↑↑	↓	↑ to ↑↑↑	-	-	↑ to ↑↑
Multi-function	↑	-	-	-	-	↑
Photo Printer	↑	- To ↑	-	- To ↑	-	-
Dot Matrix Printer	↑	↓	↓	↓	↑	-
Thermal Printer	↓	↓↓	↓	↓	-	↓↓
Thermal Wax	↑↑	↑↑	-	↑↑	-	-
Plotter	↑↑↑	↑↑↑	↑↑↑	↑↑	n/a	↑↑↑
* Comparisons to Inkjet *						

Figure 41: Comparison of printer features

The thermal wax and dye sublimation printers are special purpose printers. Whereas the thermal printer is a "cheap", low quality printer, the thermal wax one is just the opposite. It melts special colored wax onto the paper, making a very high quality color picture. The printer is pricey, and the cost per picture is high. Dye-sublimation printers use heat to transfer dye onto materials such as a plastic, card, paper, or fabric.

For those of you in business, occasionally you have the need to print a "large" picture or diagram or banner. Unless you do professional work at home, you will not have one of these. However there are a number of stores and internet locations that have them and will do the work at a reasonable price.

3-D printers are a relatively new product. Hobbyists can buy inexpensive ones that produce 3-D objects from spools of plastic

Section 4: Then and Now

filament. In the manufacturing world they have found a place, providing an important tool to make many of our products (even the 2013 Americas Cup sailboat used this technology). Let's think about another use. Suppose you are up in the space station, 254 miles above the earth and a hinge on one of your research devices breaks. Do you just get in your space shuttle and make a quick trip to your local hardware store? I don't think so! But, if you had a 3-D printer, you could have NASA send you the file and make one yourself.

Figure 42: A 3-D printer

There are printers that print on objects other than paper. Although it is unlikely that you will have these special printers at home (unless you are in the business), you can go to the Internet to get your favorite picture printed on a T-Shirt, a coffee mug, or a cake.

20: Mobile is Noble

Let's look and see what mobile devices we have. Where's the pager? It's gone, gone the way of the dinosaur. And the PDA, extinct! What replaced them? The Smartphone!

Not that long ago we had devices to do one purpose. An iPod or MP3 player played music. A GPS gave you driving directions. A camera took pictures. A Camcorder took movies. A cell phone was a phone.

Section 4: Then and Now

Now a Smartphone does it all. Maybe not as good as a device intended for a particular function, but more than acceptable. Apps, programs for mobile devices, have become part of today's vocabulary. Since they are application programs, I have to double or triple my count when I mention the number of application programs available today.

Mobile Phone Features (90's vs today)

- Phone
- Camera (primitive)
- Phone numbers

- Phone
- Camera(s)
- Addresses
- GPS
- Music
- Games
- Apps
- Internet
- E-Book Reader

Now we are in the age of mobile devices. Before, we had cell phones, Laptops, and not much in between. Now we have smartphones, E-Book readers, tablets, notepads, and laptops.

As you can see, there is a range of offerings from small smartphones to larger ones, small tablets, larger tablets, notebooks, and laptops of all sizes, processing power, and features (like memory and secondary storage).

These devices come with cameras and speakers. The cameras produce a reasonable image, especially useful for making these devices a videophone. Whereas the tiny sized speakers of previous years would only produce what could pass for music, today's ones produce reasonable sound. If you want more, you can buy headphones or audio systems of great to excellent quality.

21: Digital Cameras

Our evolutionary tree that looked pretty sparse during its infancy in the 80's is now well developed with an impressive canopy. But real trees produce fruit or seeds that germinate and produce another tree. So did our tree. We now have a camera tree.

Film cameras have been around for over 150 years. In their prime you needed separate cameras for different purposes. If you wanted to take movies, you had to buy a movie camera. If you wanted panoramic pictures, you bought a panoramic camera. Now digital cameras and smartphones do all of these.

When the digital camera first came out, its resolution was 640 X 480 pixels (.3 Megapixels). It was a nice toy, but serious photographers felt it was just that and that it would never challenge the film camera.

Section 4: Then and Now

Now a digital camera with 20 Megapixels or more is common. They are instruments of choice for most professionals. They ARE computers. They contain hardware and software inside them to process the picture as it is being taken.

One example is digital zoom. Digital zoom is a way of making the picture bigger by enlarging it inside the camera without using any more pixels. Normally not a desired approach, it works acceptably if you have a camera with a large number of Megapixels and don't zoom too much. Even if Your 20 Megapixel picture is now reduced to a 5 Megapixel resolution, it still looks fine.

Even the 200" telescope at Mt. Palomar now uses a digital camera – with 240 Megapixel resolution.

Figure 43: Some digital cameras

Complementing them are the software applications that enable amateurs and professionals alike to edit and enhance photographs. You can now do the same type of picture editing that a professional photographer could do in a darkroom.

22: Where am I? – The GPS

In the early 90's the first GPS's became available for commercial use. A GPS uses signals from satellites to determine your position. Now you could consult a device to know exactly where you were. GPS's became prevalent as devices you could plug into your car to tell you where you were and give you driving directions. Now most cars have an option to have a built-in GPS (with a nice screen). But suppose you are walking or on your bike? There are now GPS's that you can strap on your wrist. Civilian GPS's are currently accurate to within a few feet (military ones are more accurate). If you have a Smartphone, you can easily get driving instructions. Current GPS's show you a map and talk to you.

Did you know that a requirement of all cell phones that they have GPS capability? Your service provider will not connect an old one if it doesn't have this feature.

Treasure hunters must love them. Before GPS's if they found a treasure ship, and had to leave because of treacherous weather, they might not find it again. Now, as long as the ship didn't move, they can get exactly to the location.

23: Operating Systems

Software has evolved as fast and significantly as hardware. Operating Systems on Mainframes, Servers and PC's are a big part of these changes.

In 2001 IBM replaced its older operating system with z/OS, a 64 bit operating system

Microsoft Windows has gone from Windows 95 to Windows 10 (in almost a dozen releases).

Section 4: Then and Now

Did you know that when you buy a new PC / laptop, part of its price goes to Microsoft for the cost of "Windows?"

UNIX, which has been around since the late 60's has given birth to Linux. Linux is an open-source product. That means not only is it free, but enthusiasts can obtain the source code and modify or enhance it. It runs on any PC or laptop that will support Windows.

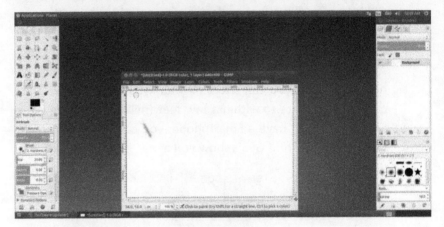

Figure 44: Linux

Linux comes with a collection of applications that meets the needs of most users. What do most casual users need or want?

- A way to browse the Internet (the WWW)
- A way to send / read E-Mail
- A way to look at and edit pictures
- A way to listen to music
- A word processor
- Games

A brand new O/S has appeared, Android. All these new Smartphones and tablets need an O/S. They need something with user friendliness and multi-tasking, but not as complicated and unwieldly as Windows 10.

On the apple side of the house IOS, a mobile operating system developed for apple hardware made its appearance in 2007. It is used in Apple smartphones and iPads.

O/S FEATURES

	MS Windows	Mac OS	IOS	Linux / UNIX	Android
Cut/copy/paste	√	√	√	√	√
Shortcuts	√	√			
File Linking		√		√	
File permissions		√		√	
Files Case Sensitive				√	
Multiple Users	√	√		√	
Software download App.			√	√	√

Table 6: O/S Features

An O/S like tool that can be used in today's PC's and laptops is the "Virtual Machine." This is an application program that looks like a computer to the Operating System running under it. Thus you can be running your O/S (Like Windows 10) and under it be running Linux or Windows XP. Just like switching between applications like Excel and Word, you can switch between Excel and Linux.

Section 4: Then and Now

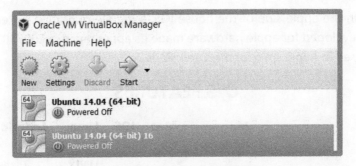

Figure 45: VMWare Virtual Machine

FAT, FATTER, No FAT – How operating systems organize data on the hard disk

The original PC had a 10 megabyte hard drive. It used a File Allocation Table (FAT) to show the O/S where the files were located on the disk. The original FAT16 was replaced by the FAT32, allowing for larger disk drives and more efficient use of space.

With the introduction of Windows XP, a new file system type became available, NTFS. Among other things, NTFS provided an option to compress a disk drive, saving space.

Linux currently uses the EXT3 and EXT4 file systems.

There are utilities that let you convert from one file system type to another. The Microsoft "Convert" program is a command line program that will convert one file system type to another.

```
C:\Users\Marc>convert /?
Converts a FAT volume to NTFS.

CONVERT volume /FS:NTFS [/V] [/CvtArea:filename] [/NoSecurity] [/X]

  volume        Specifies the drive letter (followed by a colon),
                mount point, or volume name.
  /FS:NTFS      Specifies that the volume will be converted to NTFS.
  /V            Specifies that Convert will be run in verbose mode.
  /CvtArea:filename
                Specifies a contiguous file in the root directory
                that will be the place holder for NTFS system files.
  /NoSecurity   Specifies that the security settings on the converted
                files and directories allow access by all users.
  /X            Forces the volume to dismount first if necessary.
                All open handles to the volume will not be valid.

C:\Users\Marc>
```

Not all O/S's work with all file system types. Linux understands FAT and NTFS file systems as well as its own file system types, but Windows does not understand Linux file system types (without special software). My car music player reads FAT32 flash drives but not NTFS ones.

24: More Software Tools

There are now many, many thousands of application programs. They now span the platforms from PC's and Mac's to Smartphones and tablet to TV's and automobiles. We use the term "apps" for application programs on portable devices. Many times an application (like LibreOffice) may run on a number of platforms[7].

With picture taking being as accessible as your smartphone or tablet, a way of editing these pictures easily becomes more important. We need software tools. Let's take an analogy. In my pocket I have a penknife. It has a few knives, a screwdriver, and a scissors. I can tighten a screw, cut a piece of paper, and slice pieces out of some wood. If I need more, I have a tool bag in my closet. It has screwdrivers, a hammer, a few wrenches, and some pliers. I can do a few simple repairs with it. In my workroom I

---

[7] A platform is the combination of the computer's hardware and its Operating System.

Section 4: Then and Now

have a reasonable set of tools including saws, drills, etc. If I need some professional tools, I go to my neighbor.

The same is true for picture editing tools. Your smartphones, tablets, or cameras have some simple tools for editing pictures. PC's and laptops have better editing tools like "Microsoft Paint" that let you do simple editing of pictures, like cropping and changing the contrast. Other programs provide more features and are slightly harder to use. Even fancier programs provide features that would have required a photographic darkroom in the days of film cameras. They may require more skill to use them, but can produce professional results.

One aspect of these is that once you edit your picture, save it and exit from the program, the changes are permanent - you cannot undo them.

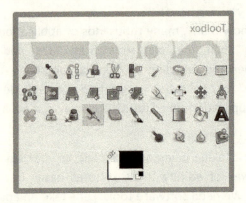

Figure 46: A Photo Editing Program Toolbox

Vector graphics programs draw objects like squares, circles, arrows and text on the screen. Unlike raster graphics programs, any object can be moved, resized, or removed. LibreOffice Draw is a freeware program with many features to create graphical pages. PowerPoint can also create slides with shapes, lines and pictures that can be edited like the above programs.

Section 4: Then and Now

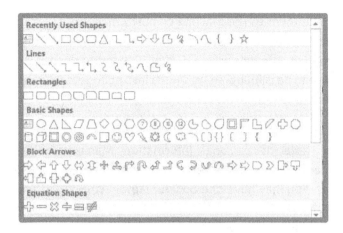

Figure 47: Available PowerPoint Shapes

Scanners convert hardcopy pictures and text into computer "image" files. The common format is: ".jpg", a standard format for pictures. It IS a picture file. Most picture editing programs provide a way to acquire a picture from a scanner.

The interface that these programs use to interface with a scanner is called a TWAIN interface (Technology Without An Interesting Name).

If you scan in a page from a document, it is a picture of that page. Suppose you want to edit that page. You need another tool, a program that does Optical Character Recognition (OCR). These programs convert the picture file into a text file. Depending on the quality of the OCR program and the legibility of the text, the OCR program may do well or poorly in the conversion (𝕳𝖔𝖜 𝖌𝖔𝖔𝖉 𝖆𝖗𝖊 𝖞𝖔𝖚 𝖎𝖓 𝖗𝖊𝖆𝖉𝖎𝖓𝖌 𝖙𝖍𝖎𝖘 𝖙𝖊𝖝𝖙?). Smartphones often have OCR software so that you can take a picture of some text and convert it to text.

Let's go back a few years. I have to pay some bills. I write out the checks. I have to pay a little money to buy some pieces of paper to put them in – envelopes. I have to pay more money to buy some other pieces of paper with sticky stuff on them – stamps,

Section 4: Then and Now

then take them to the mailbox or post office. Now I just call up my banking app on my Smartphone or tablet, login, and enter the information. The bills are paid. Plus, if I want to deposit a check, all I have to do is follow some simple instructions to take a picture of it and have it deposited. No running to the bank.

Apps, Apps, Lets Sync Them Here

In the area of Personal Information Managers, tools like calendars, address books and to-do lists may exist on several devices. You may have one on your laptop, your tablet and your Smartphone. How do you keep them synchronized? Many apps do have "sync" capabilities. This means that if you modify the calendar on your PC, your Smartphone will soon have the change(s). Note, there must be a network connections between the devices for them to synch. You can also sync with others who have the same User ID.

25: Robots

Robots have snuck onto the scene, unnoticed by most people. That's because our concept of a robot is a humanoid construction made out of metal with two arms, two legs, a torso, and a head. It talks with a definite "robotic" sound.

In reality, robots have been a part of our world for many years. If you own a car, its welding and painting was done by robots. More and more of the assembly process is now being done by robots. Some automobile companies even have robots to insert and install the seat through the door opening. Below are some robots. The one on the left may be a well-known one, "Robbie the Robot" from the 1956 movie, Forbidden Planet (I cheated, because it is not a real robot). Next is one used for welding, followed by a real humanoid one.

Figure 48: Robots

If you want your floors cleaned without having to hire a cleaning service or do it yourself, you buy a robot.

If you were a SWAT team member and there was a possible heavily armed terrorist in the building, would you rather go in there yourself or send in a robot?

Another robotic device is the "drone." A drone is an aircraft without a human pilot.

Although most robots are "usiform"[8], some are designed to look like people. There are some that you wouldn't know they were robots if you were a dozen feet away. They also talk better than some people I know.

---

[8] A term taken from an old science fiction story where humanoid robots were redesigned to only have the features needed to do their specific job.

93

Section 4: Then and Now

26: Are Computers Smart?

I won't get into the exact definition of what "smart" is. However let's look at what's happened recently. About 20 years ago a computer beat the best chess player (and now our computers are hundreds of times faster). Not that long ago a computer beat the world's best "go" player, a game by many people to be harder than chess.

We have self-driving cars. As of this time four states have legalized them and legislation is being considered in a number of other states. Even though I know about software bugs and that self-driving cars may have a few, I would still trust them over many of the human drivers on the road.

Recently a computer passed the "Turing Test." It was developed by Alan Turing in 1950, to test a computer's ability to exhibit intelligent behavior equivalent to, or indistinguishable from, that of a human. Turing proposed that a human evaluator would judge a person's conversation with a computer and with another person. The evaluator would be aware that one of the two is a computer, and all participants would be separated from one another. The conversation would be limited to text-only, so the result would not depend on the machine's ability to render words as speech. If the evaluator cannot reliably tell the machine from the human, the machine is said to have passed the test.

Another recent example of computer intelligence was demonstrated when "Watson", a computer developed by IBM beat two of the best players in the history of the TV Jeopardy show.

I am reminded of the story about a lady who went into a fish market and told the owner, "I heard that fish heads are a brain food. I'd like to buy some." Knowing he had a live one, he sold her a dozen fish heads at five dollars each. Every week she would come in and buy more. Finally after about a month she asked,

94

"How come I'm paying five dollars for a fish head when you're selling the whole fish for five dollars?" He replied, "See how much smarter you're getting."

Will computers become "self-aware"- That's where the computer is aware of its own existence? I don't know, but some scientists feel that it's not a question of if, but one of when.

27: Big things come in small (inexpensive) packages

The smartphone is an extremely important part of today's life. It does many things besides just being a phone. But it is NOT a general purpose computer. Imagine if I had to write this book using a smartphone. A laptop is ideal for this, powerful and small, but not inexpensive.

Let's talk about the Raspberry Pi. The Raspberry Pi is about the size of a pack of cigarettes. I purchased some accessories with mine (like a camera) so the cost was about $60. It uses a micro-SD card for storage. Mine has a 64 Giga-byte one and I multi-boot several O/S's (all variations of Linux).

Figure 49: Raspberry Pi

It uses a standard micro-USB charger for power and connects via an HDMI cable to a TV. It has 4 USB ports for mouse and keyboard connectivity and built-in WI-FI.

Section 4: Then and Now

It can do all the things that a typical user might want to do: Surf the internet, send E-Mail, look at and edit pictures and play music. I can even develop software on it using GAMBAS.

I just ran across a new retro gadget, the C-64 Mini. It is a 50% scale replica and features HDMI output, a classic style joystick and   64   built-in   games.

Section 4: Then and Now

Some aspects of computer science are independent of time (well, somewhat). Networking has been a part of system design for over forty years. Good project management procedures have been around forever (or so it seems).

Figure 50: Some Dinosaurs

28: The Internet, the World Wide Web and Networking

The Internet:

In modern history certain inventions have drastically changed the way we live. Electricity, the automobile, and television are a few. Few if any of us remember the time before these inventions; we take them for granted. Let's add the Internet; some of us remember the time before it existed. It first came into existence in the late 60's. But, what is it?

Let's start with an analogy. Suppose you pick up your house phone (those phones that are NOT wireless) and call your aunt who lives a few states away. After a short time you get connected. What happened was that your phone made a connection to your local central office. Your local central office made the connection to your aunt's central office and then your aunt's phone through a sophisticated network. You don't know (or care) whether it used microwave towers, satellites, fiberglass cables or something else.

The internet is similar. Your modem/router connects you to your Internet Service Provider (ISP). From there the packets are routed through the network to the destination. You don't know (or care) whether it used microwave towers, satellites, fiberglass cables or something else. Just like your office may have its own PBX, Your home/office/school will probably have its own Local Area Network (LAN).

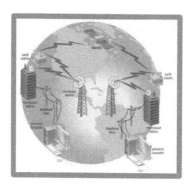

Figure 51: The Global Network

The World Wide Web (WWW):

The World Wide Web and the Internet are NOT the same things. The WWW uses the internet to allow PC's and smart devices to

97

access data on web Servers. The WWW uses Hyper Text Transfer Protocol to allow nodes to talk to each other. The language they use is Hypertext Meta Language (HTML)

A Browser is not a Dog:

A browser is a program that talks to web Servers. All browsers provide similar functionality. They all allow the user to enter the URL (web address) of the web site to be accessed. This information is sent to the web Server specified by the URL. The server finds the web page requested and sends it to the browser. The browser then formats the data and puts it on the screen. All browsers understand HTML.

Modern browsers allow you to talk to a number of web sites by using tabs. By selecting the proper tab, you can talk to that web site. Microsoft and Apple each have their own browsers (Internet Explorer- replaced by Microsoft Edge and Safari respectively). In addition, ones like Google Chrome and Mozilla Firefox have versions for most platforms.

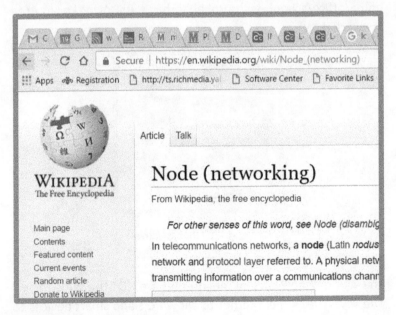

Section 4: Then and Now

Browsers have the concept of bookmarks or favorites (the same thing). You can bookmark a web site (or web page) that you are interesting in viewing later and go to that place later.

You can even copy that set of bookmarks to another browser by exporting them from one browser and importing them using the other browser. The browsers can be on the same computer or on different computers or even different platforms.

As yet another analogy, suppose you are at a cocktail party. You drift over to a group of duplicate bridge players. They are talking about support doubles and South African Transfer bids. They are talking English, but you have absolutely no idea what they are talking about. You then move to a group of Astronomers talking shop. They are talking about event horizons and singularities. Again, they are talking English, but you are at a loss to understand them.

Browsers all understand the basic language – HTML. However if the web page contains certain extensions to HTML, the browser may not display the information properly. That's why some web sites specify certain browsers since they know that these browsers will display the contents of their web pages properly.

A Search Engine doesn't need gas

The Internet started in the late 60's with four sites; the World Wide Web in the late 90's. Now there are over a half billion Web sites. These sites may have items for sale (almost anything), historical information, and scientific information; almost anything you may be interested in finding out about.

How do you find something? We have a new phrase that has entered our language: "Google it." Google is just one of the popular search engines. A Search Engine finds and catalogs information on the web. How it does this is "Beyond the scope of

Section 4: Then and Now

this book" (remember my comment on this earlier in the book). You put in the word or phrase you are looking for and the search engine returns a list of sites containing the word or phrase. Although the information it contains is almost mind boggling, it only contains information about a small portion of the WWW. Imagine how much information is just contained in the Library of Congress.

Libraries have access to information not available to most search engines. Suppose you wanted information from the May 12th 1945 issue of Newsweek.

You may falsely assume that the information you see is accurate (If you do, look for comments by Dr. Marc Lipman on my web site. I just became a medical doctor yesterday by putting it on my site). The information may be outdated, incomplete, or just plain wrong.

Sometimes a word or phrase returns too many answers. I was looking for a wrecked ship, The Caterina. Unfortunately there was a passenger by that name on the Titanic. I got much too many hits. I was able to tell the search engine that I wanted information that contained "Caterina" but not "Titanic".

Networks:

Networking is a way of connecting computers, computer-like devices and peripherals together. Individuals may have a Home Area Network. It connects their PC's, laptops, printers, and smart devices together. Now if you have a printer connected to a computer on your network, you can print to it from any other computer. You still have to have that computer turned on. But if you have a printer connected to your network, you can print to it from any device connected to the network (hardwired or WI-FI). Many computers can be hardwired to the network or connected via WI-FI.

A business or school may have a Local Area Network (LAN), connecting its devices together.

These networks are almost always connected to the Wide Area Network (WAN).

Packets:

The networks we will be discussing use a protocol called "TCP/IP." TCP/IP uses the concept that a message is sent from one point (a node) to another in the form of packets – packages of information. The message may need only one packet or many packets. When these packets reach their destination, they are assembled to produce the original message. Not all packets may follow the same path as shown below.

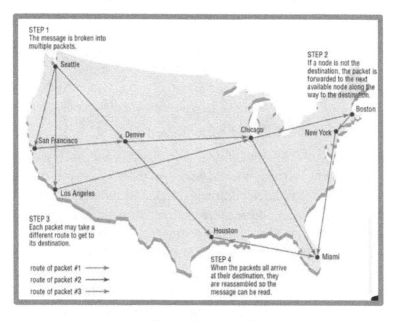

Figure 53: How Packets are Routed

There is information built into each packet to tell where it came from, where it is going to, and information so that the receiving end knows that the message was received properly. The same concept works whether the message is a file going from your PC

Section 4: Then and Now

to your WI-FI connected printer or a file coming from a web site in China. Since the packets may be routed through a number of intermediate nodes, the time taken may be much longer than the time for the message to go through a LAN. I knew of a case where the time for a large set of files going from New Jersey to Colorado took twenty times as long.

Just like the destination for your phone call has a destination number, so do packets. This destination is called an IP Address. It consists of four octal digits separated by periods (e.g. 192.168.1.1). Just like your phone number is unique, so are IP Addresses. Its concept is similar to telephone numbers where your office number has an area code followed by the central office number followed by your office number followed by your extension number.

The IP address above has a special meaning. It is the address of your router (if you have one). If you enter that address into your browser, you will be connected to it. If you know its ID and password, you can look at its settings and do things such as change your WI-FI password.

Do you know the telephone number of your best friend? Probably not. In today's world with smartphones, we rely on our address books and don't worry about phone numbers. The same is true for Internet address. We have Uniform Resource Locators (URL's). URL's are like a person's name in an address book. When I want to look at the web site for the Barnegat Light Historical Society, I simply enter: "http://www.bl-hs.org." The "www" specifies that it is on the World Wide Web. The "bl-hs.org" is the name of the web site. The ".org" specifies that it is a tax free organization. Because I didn't enter a specific web Page name, I get the home page. Note, the "http:// "specifies: Hyper Text Transfer Protocol and is optional. Although the suffix usually tells you what type of site it is, there doesn't seem to be anyone policing it.

Section 4: Then and Now

Common suffixes:

- .com: commercial
- .edu: An educational institute
- .gov: state and national government
- .int: International organizations
- .mil: U.S. Military
- .net: Network
- .org: Organization (usually non-profit)

If I had entered "http://www.bl-hs.org/about_the_museum.htm", I would have gotten the "about_the_museum.htm" web page.

The concept of packets also explains how the 3-in-1 package that many people have works. For those who don't know about it, it is a package offered by cable companies and other ISP's that provide TV, telephone and internet for one price. The customer may have one or more TV's and some of them may have "on-demand" (a feature that allows them to view a specific program). Suppose one person is watching an "on-demand" movie, another a regular TV channel, another surfing the Internet, and a fourth one on the phone. Why doesn't everything get confused: PACKETS! Each of the modems for these devices have a unique IP Address. Even though all the packets arrive at the modems, they throw out the ones that are not for them and send the ones that are to the device.

The concept also explains why we sometimes see slow Internet response. If there is not much traffic through the cable connecting you to your ISP, the packets arrive with no problems. However, if there is heavy traffic, packets collide. One has to wait while the other is re-sent. This slows things down. This is why some people notice that their Internet speed is faster at 3:00 AM than at 7:00 PM.

Section 4: Then and Now

Connections and Bandwidth:

Home users often have a choice of ways to connect to the Internet. The most common is Cable. If a cable company provides service to your area, you can get Internet service through them. If you are in an area with FIOS support, you can use it. If your residence has an area open to the sky, you can get satellite service. If you are within a reasonable distance from the telephone central office, DSL may be a choice. Sometimes you only have one choice. Jackrabbit, Arizona (if you are traveling on the Interstate and blink, you may miss it) has only one choice - satellite. If you live in a more populated area, you may have a few choices of ISP's. Some may give you bandwidth choices. If all you are doing is handling E-Mail and browsing the Internet, any bandwidth may do. If you are downloading movies or uploading large picture files, more bandwidth may be needed. Often the bandwidth provided by an ISP has a faster download speed that the upload speed (there are exceptions). This is because people usually download more data than they upload - you enter: "www. Mysite.com" (a few characters) and a whole web page comes down).

Bluetooth is not a dental condition

WI-FI gives you access to a Local Area Network (often your Home Area Network). From there you can connect to devices on the network, or anywhere if your network has Internet access. There is another wireless standard – Bluetooth. Bluetooth lets you connect your audio device to a Smartphone, tablet, or even your laptop. The device may be headphones, speakers, or often your car. A simple setup is required. The distance is shorter than with WI-FI – usually about 33 feet. It is NOT as secure as WI-FI, so be careful when using it in places like a shopping mall.

Snail-Mail -> E-Mail

UNIX has had E-Mail for over forty years. You could create a text message and send it to any user on that system or to a user on any UNIX system that your system knew about. It used modems and telephone lines to connect to remote systems. Now with the internet we can send E-Mail to anyone in the world – in a matter of minutes.

Some E-Mail applications are resident on your PC. The E-Mails are downloaded to them from the Internet and you can read them at any time (no Internet required).

Most E-Mail applications are resident on the Internet. You use your browser to access them. Their advantage is that you can access your E-Mail anywhere that you can get to the Internet, with a PC, laptop, or mobile device.

You can attach files to your e-Mail. These attachments can be pictures, documents, or other types of files (many E-Mail systems have a limit on the size of your uploads). Remember that the user on the receiving end must have software that reads that type of file for it to be useful. It does no good to send an Excel spreadsheet to a user who doesn't have a spreadsheet program on their device. The E-Mail systems I use have spelling checkers and formatting capabilities.

There are some important things to consider when using E-Mail. E-Mail is NOT private. Employers usually have access to your E-Mail. Always use proper language in E-Mails. Avoid sending E-Mail to people who don't need to read it; it wastes their time.

Somebody I know received an E-Mail from a co-worker referring to a client as a certain part of a horse's anatomy. The client was on the E-Mail's: copy-to list.

It's Cloudy

In the prehistoric days – after dinosaurs but before WI-FI – If you wanted to move data somewhere else, you put it on a floppy diskette or CD and took it with you. That's what I would have done if I wanted to work on this book with my friend. But, he lives a few states away. Now, all I have to do is use the "Cloud". As long as we can both get on the Internet, we can look at the document together. If I make a correction, he sees it immediately, and vice-versa. Now collaboration is only a URL away.

I can also put documents, pictures, and other data that I want to share with others, on the Cloud. Currently all the sites I use require me to specify whom I want to share these items with.

There are a number of organizations that offer storage on the Cloud. Many devices like Smartphones provide easy access to the Cloud.

29: Is there a doctor in the house? – Computers in Medicine

Both general purpose computers and special purpose computers have greatly enhanced the medical profession. As in many other professions and businesses, computers help run the day-to-day business.

Electronic Medical Records (EMR's) are becoming a standard with many systems available for small practices to large ones. Paper is being replaced by electronics in all aspects of the profession. Epocrates, a program that runs on PC's and mobile devices, provides detailed information about drugs to doctors and other health care professionals, replacing the need for them to keep and update written information. It even shows pictures of the pills so that a patient who doesn't remember the name of the drug can identify it.

Most diagnostic devices like Cat Scanners and MRI's contain special purpose computers. At the dentist's office and diagnostic clinics, X-rays using film are being replaced by sensors feeding into computers (using USB connections). There are even a number of robotic devices that perform surgery.

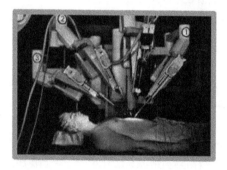

If I covered all the computer devices associated with the medical field, I would probably double the size of this book.

30: Maintaining your Computer

Let's Backup a Bit

You may remember Murphy's Law: "Anything that can happen will happen." I have a corollary to it: "It will happen at the worst possible moment." The common time for people to realize that they should do backups is when their computer dies an hour before it is time to print their term paper.

People ask me, "When or what should I backup?" My response is, "WHAT IS YOUR LEVEL OF PAIN IF YOUR DATA IS LOST?" In very few situations nothing is required. My friend has a second computer (actually his fourth). He only uses it to browse the web. He does not save anything on it. If the hard drive fails, he throws the computer away. No backups are required. This is an exception!

The first step is to make sure you have a backup of your O/S. Manufactures often put a backup of the O/S on the "D:" drive. But this is still on the same physical hard drive. If that fails, you are in big trouble! The O/S's that I know of have tools to back up your O/S. You can use DVD's (you need many of them) or another drive. An external hard drive is a good choice. Now, if you need to repair an O/S problem, or even put it back onto another drive to replace a bad one, you have the data.

Now that we have taken care of the big one, let's turn to other items. I was thinking about a Psychology Professor who brought a big glass beaker into the classroom and put it on the lectern. "This represents life!" he stated. He then preceded to fill it up with golf balls. "This represents the important things in life such as your health and your family!" He then added marbles, filling up the spaces between the golf balls. "This represents the less important things in life such as your job and your house!" He then poured sand into the beaker, filling up the spaces. "This represents the minutia in your life, the little things that you deal with!" He then opened two bottles of beer and poured them into the beaker. "This shows you. No matter how full your life is, you always have time for a few beers!"

For the more important things, you probably should make more than one backup. Putting a backup in a separate physical location

Section 4: Then and Now

is a good idea. Suppose your house burns down! If your data is backed up to the Cloud; it's good, that won't burn down. If things are automatically backed up to the Cloud, that's also good.

External hard drives, flash drives, and DVD's are also good for backup. Which one you use depends on the size of the data you are backing up. Your pictures of your last vacation may easily fit on a flash drive, but your entire collection of music may not. Buying an external hard drive just to back up your Word documents may be overkill. Upload speed and cost for Cloud storage may affect your decision to keep everything there. I personally use a combination of all of these. When thinking about backups, think about all the devices that you have data on. Your Smartphone and tablet are good candidates. Don't worry about items that are synched between devices. Don't worry about software that you can easily download from the Internet. Do worry about items that you paid for and will have to pay again if you have to download them again.

Repair, Upgrade, or Replace???

Sometimes a student will ask me, "I have an older computer. Should I replace it?" The question of replace it, upgrade it, or keep the old one is not an easy question to answer. I start by answering the question with a question(s). "How old is your computer? Is it working? Is it a desktop or a laptop? What do you use it for?"

Let's look at extremes. If you have plenty of money, replace it. If it is a 5 year old or older laptop and it is not working – a bad motherboard, you probably should replace it. If it is working and all you use it for is basic things such as surfing the Internet, sending E-Mail and writing documents, keep it.

Otherwise it gets a lot more complicated. If you are running short of disk space, a portable drive that you plug in using your USB port may be a good solution. They are relatively inexpensive and can also be used with other computers and mobile devices. Similarly, an external DVD player / recorder can resolve issues with a bad internal one. Extra memory (RAM) is inexpensive and easy to install. Be careful, if Your PC / laptop has all its memory slots used you may have to buy more memory than you expected. For example, if you have 2 memory slots with two 2 GB memory cards (4 GB), and you want 8 GB, you probably will have to remove them and replace them with two 4 GB modules. If you have a spare slot, you can just buy one 4 GB module.

A bad internal hard drive can sometimes be replaced at a reasonable cost, a possible solution if your computer is only a few years old. Remember, you have to reinstall the O/S (did you back it up?).

Earlier I discussed how hardware has evolved through the years. If you are thinking about doing it yourself, remember this: A circuit board designed for today's computer will probably not work in a ten year old computer, and vice-versa. An EISA hard disk drive from your 10 year old computer will probably not work in your new desktop. Memory from a Dell computer will probably not work in your HP computer (it probably won't even fit). Do the proper research before trying to match parts. USB devices are interchangeable. The only caveat is that a CD/DVD burner may not be able to copy disks at its high speed if you are connecting it to a computer with a slower type of USB.

Software problems can often be resolved at a reasonable cost (especially if you have a friend who is computer literate.) However, buying a new O/S may not cost that much less than buying a new PC with a new O/S.

I am reminded of a time when some managers who worked for a computer company were on a business trip. Their rental car got a flat tire. The Sales Manager stated, "We need a new car." The

Section 4: Then and Now

Service Manager replied, "Let's just interchange a few parts. That should work." The Software Manager asserted, "Just turn it off and turn it on again. That should solve the problem!"

Keeping your software up-to-date

When you get a new operating system or software package, you can be reasonably assured that there are no software or security problems – If you believe that, I have a bridge to sell you!

Different systems have different approaches to software maintenance. Microsoft Windows uses the "Service Pack" one. A Service Pack contains bug fixes, security fixes, and sometimes a few minor improvements (big changes are reserved for a newer version of the operating system or software package).

Ubuntu Linux has a Software Updater (under the System Tools / Administration menu). It searches for all software changes and allows you to download and install any / all changes. Portable devices also provide updates to their software...

Sometimes a software package has a newer version that you can download for free from the web. It is usually a combination of bug fixes and new features.

I personally recommend keeping up with the latest changes. Sometimes they may not affect your specific product (How many of you have a RAID unit in your PC). But why take chance. All it costs you is the time for it to download and install.

What Platform are you on?

Remember that a platform is the combination of your device's hardware and operating system. Currently there are 5 common platforms in use for computers and mobile devices.

- Windows, which runs on PC's and laptops is the most common one in the United States.

111

- MAC OS runs on Apple PC's and Apple laptops
- Linux which runs on PC's, laptops and some devices like the Raspberry PI is not as common, but free.
- Android, which runs on tablets and Smartphones is a popular one.
- IOS, a product for Apple mobile devices rounds out the assortment.

They all have a graphical User Interface, are easy to use, and support a large number of application programs.

Out With the Old – Carefully

In the world of paper documents, we sometimes get rid of old ones. If it is something like tax records, we are careful since they may have sensitive information like social security numbers. Getting rid of computer equipment poses similar dangers. The files on your old disk drive may contain sensitive information. If your computer is used for business purposes, it may contain information that competitors would love to get a hold of.

Why not just erase all the files? Files are stored on sectors on the disk. Erasing the files does NOT erase the sector(s) contents, only the pointers to them. There are special programs that will erase your disk completely. Consider using one of them. Another way is to take tools like a hammer and sandpaper. A nicely sanded disk platter is not readable.

If you have a hard disk failure, there are companies that can often recover its contents – AT A PRICE!

Think about other devices. Your tablet and your Smartphone may also have sensitive information (how about your watch?). Even your car may be suspect. How about its' GPS? Does it have your house address or the addresses of your friends or family? If it has Bluetooth, does it have phone numbers that you wouldn't like others to see? Some cars have a chip containing this information that you can remove.

31: Projects

A major part of software development is implementing projects. It may be a simple one that takes a person a week or so to complete, or one that takes a team of developers months or more.

Implementing projects involving computer systems requires formal and controlled procedures if you want it to turn out right.

As you read this you'll see that these same procedures apply whether it is building a computer system or building a bridge.

This set of procedures is called the "Systems Development Life Cycle." It consists of the following steps:

1. Preliminary investigation

2. Systems analysis

3. Systems design

4. Systems development

5. Systems implementation

6. Systems maintenance

- Information systems are frequently revised and upgrade

I am going to use two examples here, a small one and a medium sized one. We'll see that the same methods and procedures apply, though not quite as formally for the small one.

The small one has to do with "Number 1 Son", who sometimes has to make health presentations to school children. Background

113

music is a highly desirable aspect of the show. However, requiring a sound person to control it is NOT highly desirable. Hence the question, "Dad, can you design a program that runs on a laptop and controls the music, using a remote mouse to do this?" This was the start of the "Remote Music Manager".

The medium sized one relates to a company that markets telephone systems. It provides service contracts for their systems. If a customer has a problem with a telephone, they call the support number and a technician comes and replaces the defective one with a refurbished one and removes the old one. The bad one is sent to the repair center where it is junked or repaired. But how do they decide to junk it or repair it? They needed a state-of-the-art computer system (The Repair Planning System) to replace an old one that was to be discarded.

Both started out with a study of the existing system (or lack thereof). The Systems Analyst (me in these cases) may know little or nothing about the customer's business needs at the start. But, learning a lot about it is a necessity. Written requirements are essential to the process; only a page or two for the first one and many pages for the second one. Often the user does not know exactly what he/she wants. The Systems Analyst may have to help them describe in detail what they want. All parties signing off on the requirements ensures that there is no ambiguity in what the customer wants.

Sometimes a software solution may NOT be cost effective. I knew of one situation where a city government manager asked an analyst to investigate a software solution for a system to process and pay certain vendors. As it turned out, a member of the department would do this once a month on her lunch hour.

The buy/build decision is part of the process. Sometimes an off the shelf product will do the job at a reasonable cost. If the system has to be custom made, the cost may be high. In the

Repair Planning system, the estimate called for over a dozen developers working for about three months plus server hardware and a database system. The reader can probably get an idea of the cost. The customer must then figure out the cost / benefit of the system. If they agree, they sign off on it and work can begin. Note that the cost of the "Remote Music Manager" was a laptop and a remote mouse.

Here's something that didn't happen (because I know better). We're in the development stage of the Repair Planning System. Dates have been agreed on and work is proceeding smoothly. Mary, one of the Repair Planners calls me. "Marc, while you're doing the Adjust Schedule program, can you add a section to show repair history?" "Sure." A week later Steve, their System Planner, calls. "Marc, can you add a report by minor Business Unit?" "OK." A few days later the manager from the Repair Center asks, "Marc, Can we have a report showing what items had different repair quantities from the last week?" "OK."

June rolls around. Mel, the Repair Planning Manager, calls to confirm that the system will be ready for User Acceptance Testing next week. I tell him, "No, remember all the changes your team asked for. It'll be a few more weeks." "Wait a minute! Our written agreement calls for the system to be ready! Give me the phone number of your manager!" There goes next year's raise.

This didn't happen because part of the process is something called: "Change Management." Once the requirements have been agreed on, any requests for changes go through this process. Any and all requests are documented. The analysis includes any increases in cost and changes in delivery schedule. If the customer and the appropriate managers agree (in writing), the change will be included in the project. If they don't, the changes will not be included. They may be requested as a part of the next version of the package.

This phenomena is known as "Scope Creep." It is undesirable! I might get away with it when I am developing the Remote Music Manager for my son, but never for a major project. I have to keep it in mind when writing this book.

When I was in college, a professor I heard of decided to publish his material about programming. Chapters 8 and 9 on "Sorting and Searching" became a whole book.

Disaster Recovery – A plan for all seasons

A Disaster recovery plan is highly desirable for any project. How formal it is depends on the project.

For example, The Repair Planning System required a formal Disaster Recovery Plan including a backup computer system in another data center and off-site backup of the data.

On the other hand a student's PowerPoint project for class may not merit a written Disaster Recovery Plan, but should include periodic backing up of the file(s) on a portable medium.

Disaster Recovery is part of something we call "Contingency Planning." During our planning we have one or more brainstorming sessions. We write down anything that could happen, anything! We then determine the likelihood of the event happening and the cost in handling it. Somethings like "A Hard Drive failure" is somewhat likely and can be handled by adding a RAID unit to the server. Somethings like "The development team buying a 20 Million Dollar Lottery Ticket, winning and resigning in mass" is highly unlikely and is not worth the cost of hiring more staff, just in case.

The implementation strategy is important. It is easier if no current system exists. However, if a current one exists, you can:

- Quit running the old system and start using the new one

- *Use* both the old system and the new one side by side, until the new system has been proved reliable

- *Ph*ase in parts of the new system as parts of old one are phased out

- Have the new system tried out by a few users (Beta Testing). The good news is that they get to try the new system early. The bad news is that the new system may have bugs.

Training is very important. The users should know how to use the system, and appropriate members of the development team should be available for help[9]. Unlike one system I had to use, it is a good to train the users BEFORE the new system is implemented.

Don't forget the documentation. There are several types of documentation.

- Documentation for the people who will use the program(s). It may include user manuals and training manuals. They may be in hardcopy, on CD's, or online.

- Documentation for the computer operators, so they know how to run the program(s) and what to do if the program(s) or hardware malfunctions (if this is missing or incomplete, the developer might get a call in the middle of the night).

- Documentation for the next programmer who must modify and maintain the program (It could be you a few years later). When a program is written with appropriate comments and meaningful statements, it may be self-documenting. Note that the section below uses comments and easy to understand variable names.

---

[9] I may get grief about this from some developers.

```
' This section of code displays the sum of the
first 4 months of salary
        Dim Month As Integer
        Dim SalaryPerMonth(4) As Decimal
        Dim SalarySum As Decimal
        SalaryPerMonth(1) = 30766
        SalaryPerMonth(2) = 32366
        SalaryPerMonth(3) = 34166
        SalaryPerMonth(4) = 33765
        For Month = 1 To 4
            SalarySum = SalarySum +
SalaryPerMonth(Month)
        Next
        TextBox_TotalSalary.Text = SalarySum
```

Table 7: Example of good code

```
        Dim S1(4) As Decimal
        Dim S2 As Decimal
        S1(1) = 30766
        S2(2) = 32366
        S3(3) = 34166
        S4(4) = 33765
        For i = 1 To 4
        S2 = S2 + S1(i)
        Next
        TextBox1.Text = S2
```

Table 8: Example of bad code

Both of these programs work. However, the "bad" one would be difficult to understand and fix or upgrade. Instead of a few lines of code, imagine if there were a thousand lines of code.

Here are two scenarios that didn't really happen (well, not quite). The first one involved Pat, a developer who produced well-written, well-tested code. One week, when he was on vacation one of his programs, the "Load Comcode Usage"

118

Section 4: Then and Now

program failed due to a unique data condition. Yours truly took a look at it. The code was easy to understand and the problem easy to spot and fix. "Pat, I am sending you an E-Mail to let you know about a problem with the "Load Comcode Usage" program. I put in a fix, it is now working, and you can review it when you get back."

The other one involved Eugene, another developer whose programs "worked". One week when he was on vacation one of his programs, "The Target Inventory Level" program failed. Yours truly took a look at it. The program was so convoluted, with few comments, that I had no idea how to fix it. "Eugene, as soon as you get this voicemail, get back to the office. It is urgent that you fix it immediately! We'll talk about your vacation later"

32: Programming

History of programming

All computers execute machine language instructions. These instructions consist of binary (1's and 0's) and tell the computer what to do. VISIAC had an instruction set of 10 instructions. A large mainframe computer (like the IBM 360 – introduced in 1964) had a set of hundreds of instructions. In the old days (the 40's) the programmer had to enter the instructions into the computer's memory by hand in binary. Then in the late 40's it got better.

Assembly Language and the Assembler

Machine language programs are difficult to create and understand. Here is a piece of machine language code from VISIAC:

```
100
605
104
322
105
```

```
200
605
104
700
604
812
900
```

Do you have the slightest idea what it means?

Someone realized that they could write a program that could read in something that was more understandable to a development programmer and have the program translate it to machine language. They called it an assembler and the language assembly language. Of course, since each type of CPU has its own machine language, it would have to have its own assembly language and assembler.

Here is an example of the code for the above VISIAC program:

```
n       DATA    009
        cntr    DATA    000

        CLA     00      Initialize the counter
        STO     cntr
loop    CLA     n       If n < 0, exit
        TAC     exit
        OUT     cntr    Output a card
        CLA     cntr    Increment the card
        ADD     00
        STO     cntr
        CLA     n       Decrement n
        SUB     00
        STO     n
        JMP     loop
exit    HRS     00
```

It is still nasty, but a lot easier for the programmer to understand and use to develop programs.

High-Level Languages

However, it was still not good enough. Why couldn't someone create a language that was much easier to write in, and have a program translate it to machine language? Thus, the "Compiler" was born. We call compiler languages high level languages. Different languages were developed for different purposes. "COBOL" was developed for writing business programs. "FORTRAN" was developed for scientific programs. "BASIC" was developed as a simple language that even the novice programmer could understand and use.

Here is an example of a segment of a BASIC program:

```
For i = 1 To OutputCtr
    If Output(i, 0) <> Nothing Then
        FileWriter.WriteLine(Output(i, 0) & "," &
Output(i, 1) & Output(i, 2))
    End If
Next
FileWriter.Close()
```

There are many other general purpose languages. "C" and its variations are a powerful and efficient languages that run on most computers. They are even used to write operating systems. Some languages are tailored for a specific use. Java Script (not to be confused with Java) was developed for web pages. It runs on your client when your browser uses that web page. It can do things like tell you if your ordering information for a product is incomplete. It does NOT have any input or output commands (could you imagine what an unscrupulous web site developer could do to your computer if it had them). The only thing in the I/O arena is to read and write cookies which are harmless (that's how a web site can say: "Welcome back Marc. We haven't heard from you since ...).

The Development Process

Writing computer programs involve a "development process." The formality of this process depends on whether you are

121

working for a company developing software for a user or an individual writing a program for your son (the only time I skipped the formality was for my son).

The first step is to have a formal written Requirements Document (remember, verbal requirements aren't worth the paper they are written on!). The requirements should be approved (in writing) by all involved parties, the user, the developer, management, etc.

The next step for the developer(s) is to develop the design specifications. This is a document defining how the requirements will be met, including the inputs, outputs, processing, and the hardware and software tools needed. As with the requirements document, this document should be read and approved by all appropriate parties.

Then coding can begin. The developer writes the code (on punched cards for a mainframe computer of the 60's and 70's, or on a computer terminal for a minicomputer of that time) on a PC or terminal.

After the program is written, the developer runs the assembler or compiler program. This program produces an output report and (if there are no errors) an object file. If there are errors, the developer must correct them and go back to the coding process.

If the program assembled/compiled properly, the developer runs the program. If the program did NOT run correctly, the programmer debugs the program.

Debugging
Debugging is the process of finding and correcting program errors. Where did the term come from? Was there really a "bug"?

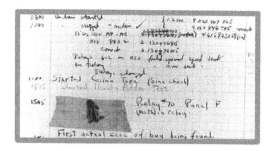

Figure 55: The First Computer Bug

Yes, programmers found a moth stuck in relay #70 of the Harvard Mark II computer in 1946 that prevented it from working correctly. Ever since then, we have used the term to describe a situation where a program does not work properly. Of course now, the "bug" is an error in the programming.

Desk Debugging

A very useful first step in debugging a program is what we call "Desk Debugging." Of course the program you wrote may work correctly the first time (You may also win the 5 Million Dollar Lottery). Take out a piece of scrap paper and start following the code, writing down intermediate results as you go. As you do this, you may see where something is wrong. Correct it and try again. When you finish doing this and everything looks good, it is time to run the program.

Breakpoints

The program may now work correctly (You may also get an agent immediately on your Help Line call). Most development tools have the ability for you to set breakpoints in your program. When the program reaches a breakpoint, it stops. You can look at the intermediate results to see if anything looks wrong. You can then correct the code and try again.

Sometimes the program never reaches the breakpoint that you expected it to. That also tells you something useful!

Section 4: Then and Now

Single Step

Another tool is the ability to run the program one step at a time. If it is an Assembler program, you are executing one machine language instruction. If it is a high-level program (such as Visual Basic), you are executing one statement in that language. At each step you look to see if the program is doing what you expected. If something unexpected occurs, you resolve the problem and rerun the program.

Error Handling

There are 3 types of program errors

- Syntax errors
- Run-time errors
- Logic errors

Syntax errors are errors in a program statement. In English "I go want to home" is incorrect syntax. Similarly in BASIC, "FIR I = 1 to 100" is incorrect syntax. The compiler or assembler will detect syntax errors.

Run-time errors are those where the program stops or produces an error message. "23 / 0" will produce a run-time error (neither a person nor a computer can divide by 0) as will trying to open a file that does not exist.

Of all the types of program errors, logic errors are often the hardest to find. The program runs, but does not produce the correct output. This is when you resort to the above debugging techniques.

When the developer finds the problem, he/she figures out the correction and goes back to the coding process. This continues until the program works properly. It is then time for testing.

Section 4: Then and Now

Testing

Testing is an involved process. There are several types of testing:

- Unit Testing
- System Testing
- Volume Testing
- User acceptance Testing
- Beta Testing

Unit testing is where the developer runs the program to see if it works correctly. He/she should not only put in the correct input and press the right buttons, but try entering bad data and pressing the wrong buttons.

Often a software product may involve a number of programs. After each individual program has been tested, the pieces are put together into a system. It is then the job of the system tester(s) to do their thing. Whereas the developer's mentality is often: "I'll test my program to make sure it works," a good system tester's mentality is: "This program HAS bugs. I'll find them!" If by some chance he/she does everything he/she can do to make the program fail and it still works, he/she reluctantly reports that the system works.

When testing a system, we usually use test data. But often we want to know if the system can handle the large amount of data that the system will be exposed to in the real world. It may take about a minute to produce a report using test data, but an hour to produce it using actual data. This may be unacceptable! In addition, real data may uncover things that the programmer or tester didn't expect.

After the development team has successfully completed all aspects of developing the system, it is time for the last step "User Acceptance Testing." The "user" tests the system to determine whether it meets the requirements (not necessarily what they wanted, but what formally asked for). In one situation, the user said, "Where's the Report by Minor Business Unit?" My response was, "Was it in the requirements?"

"Well, no"

"Then that's probably an item to put in the requirements for the next version of the system."

In some cases a company may allow some users to get a new version of a program / system before it is available to the general user community. This is called "Beta Testing." This gives the company an "extra" team of testers, who have a larger variety of hardware and uses. If a problem is found, it can be fixed before the general user community ever sees it.

A real world aspect of developing a system is to get the users involved whenever possible. Let's take scenarios A and B. In scenario A, the system was developed without any user input. In scenario B, the users saw the data editing screen, and commented on it: "Most of it is fine but here's a spot where we have to do too many steps. Can you do anything about it?" A simple change solved their problem.

In scenario A, the system went into production and the users found some problems. "We can't do our work properly! This is a bad system!" in scenario B, the system went into production and the users found some problems. "We can do some workarounds until the next release. We're satisfied."

33: Some Data Concepts

Compression

We know something about the idea of compression – shorthand. The stenographer writes down what is said in a method not known to most of us. But upon request they can read back exactly what was said. Nothing is lost.

The normal view of computer data is: one byte (8 bits) per character. This means that an "a", a "z", and a "7" all use 8 bits to represent them. In PC's this is called ASCII (American Standard Code for Information Interchange). But suppose we could use a different way to represent data. In a typical document (like this book) we use a lot more "A's" and "B's" and spaces than "Q's" and "Z's." Why couldn't we use fewer bits for the commonly used letters and more bits for the rarely used letters? So what if a "Q" used 12 bits? This is a simplistic idea of how compression works. Sometimes you can get as much as an 80% compression (you need only 20% as much space to hold your data). The real methods are more sophisticated, but this is the concept.

There are programs that compress files and folders. If you see a Microsoft file with the suffix ".zip", you know it is a compressed file. It can contain files AND folders. Thus if you want to send somebody a folder with other folders and files under it, compress it. When the person at the other end un-compresses it, they will get the folder ad its contents exactly as you sent it. Pkzip, WinZip and 7-Zip are examples of compression programs.

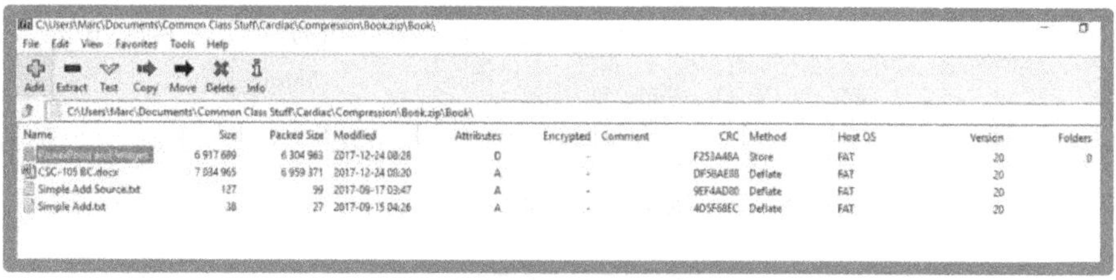

Figure 56: A Compressed folder (viewed with 7-Zip)

Modern O/S's have a compression option for the disk drives built into them. Thus if your hard drive is running out of space, you can select this option. When the hard drive saves a file, it automatically compresses it. When it loads the file, it

Section 4: Then and Now

automatically decompresses it. Your computer does a little more work processing the file, but less work moving it back and forth between the computer and the hard drive.

Lossless compression is a must for most situations. Imagine how horrible it would be if your electronic bank transfer dropped a digit or two.

However there are situations where a slight loss of data is not important. Let's take the case of pictures. If you need 3 bytes to represent each pixel for a 10 Megabyte photo, that's a lot of data. You would soon fill up your storage device. But suppose your camera could determine that two adjacent colors were very close and it could represent them as one color. A slight bit of quality is lost, but the storage saving is significant. ".JPG" files use this technique.

The same holds true for audio. A CD can hold about an hour's worth of music. But if you compress it (e.g. MP3 format) you can get about ten hours' worth of music. Of course the quality is a little less.

Examples of Compression

File Type	Size	Compressed Size	Percent of Original	Compressed Format
Text (.txt)	91,809	35,131	38%	.zip
Word Doc (.doc)	6,762,168	6,700,213	99%	.zip
PowerPoint (.ppt)	5,038,058	4,750,255	.94%	.zip

Section 4: Then and Now

Program (.exe)	248,320	110,518	45%	.zip
Picture (.bmp)	25,276,470	3,670,016	15%	.jpg
Music (audio)		2.5 MB	9%	.m4a

Table 9: Examples of Compression

Note that some types of files inherently provide a large file size saving. You may not worry if you have a large capacity storage devices. The saving may be more noticeable if you are uploading it through a slower internet connection or saving it on a small capacity storage device.

Encryption

Encryption has been around for a long time. Although I don't know when it started – perhaps soon after the alphabet was invented, but it was extremely significant in recent history. The breaking of the "ENIGMA" code was a major event in the turnaround of World War II.

The concept is simple. Suppose you replaced every "a" in your document with a "b" and every "b" with a "c." This is a primitive encryption method – easily broken. But if you get fancy enough you can come up with an encryption method that is hard to break. Some "Office" packages provide ways to encrypt your file. If someone doesn't know the password, they can't read the file. The bad news is that if you forget your password, you can't read the file yourself. The worse news is that people can buy programs that figure out the password. These programs do it by trying "A", "B", "C" and so forth. It might take them hours or even days, but sooner or later they will succeed.

Web sites may also use encryption to send and receive data. This is very important as it may contain sensitive information such as

129

a credit card number or your social security number. If the site has "HTTPS" in its address and the 🔒 symbol, it is a secured site. The data is encrypted going both ways.

Many passwords use a one-way encryption method. When I was an administrator for a UNIX computer system, I would occasionally get a call from a user, "I forgot my password. Can you give it to me?" My response was, "No!" But I can give you a new one. The way the system worked was: It would translate your password into a unique string of gobbledygook. When you logged in and supplied your password it would translate it into a string of gobbledygook. If that matched the string in your password file, you got logged in.

Data Validation

How do we know whether the data got to the other end correctly? In the old days we were not even sure whether the 8 bits of data from the memory got to the CPU correctly. They came up with the concept of parity. They added a ninth bit, called the parity bit. If "odd parity" was used, the ninth bit was set to a "1" or "0" so that if the bits were added up the result would be odd (a one).

With blocks of data they added two more bytes, a word count and a checksum. The checksum was created by adding up all the bytes and using it's negative. If the number of bytes received was not equal to the word count, something was wrong. If adding up all the bytes did not produce a zero, something was wrong.

The concept of a check digit is also used in bar codes. It uses a different algorithm but the concept is the same.

"Listen to Me"

The concept of talking to computers / robots (and having them listen) has been a staple of science fiction since its inception. Now it is commonplace in everyday life. You can now ask your

Smartphone or your car for assistance. My wife is even better than I am about getting directions and even the name of a good motel by talking to her Smartphone. Siri, Alexa, and Cortana are some digital assistants that are available today. Tabletop ones can answer your questions and even control smart home gadgets. Although these are somewhat new, by the time you read this, they may be old hat.

Help is on the Way

In the 60's, documentation was all in hardcopy format (paper). The PDP-11 assembler manual was 236 pages long. If you were a software developer you could fill up your bookshelf with manuals.

Then software companies started putting their documentation on CD's, then on the Internet. Now help is everywhere. Some products are so user friendly that minimal help is required. Between context-sensitive help (like tooltips) and easy to use buttons and text boxes, the user can easily use the product.

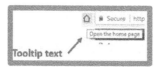

Some are intrinsically difficult to use (like a programming tool or a sophisticated paint program) and require more. On-Line help may be needed. Much documentation like tutorials and User Guides are often available on the web. If you need more help, Googling the question often gets you an answer(s). As an example, putting a picture into an Excel spreadsheet cell is not trivial. But, going on the web will get you detailed instructions.

Few writers of User Manuals get glowing praises for their work. The best that might be said is that their work is not as bad as others that you have read.

Hyperlinks, here, there, and everywhere

Most of you have used the web. After you have gotten to your home page, sometimes you have clicked your mouse on a picture or some text and gotten to another place on that page, another page on that web Site, or even another web Site. That was a hyperlink. Hyperlinks can be used in other places. A hyperlink on a Word document/spreadsheet/PowerPoint slide can direct you to another place; on the same document/worksheet/slide or to another place (a document, a spreadsheet, a PowerPoint slide, or a place on the web.

PDF files are pretty damn fine

I lost the directions of how to set my digital watch. I bought a slightly used motorcycle that didn't come with an Owner's Manual. I am working on my income taxes and I need another tax form. My new car's owner manual doesn't have all the information I need. What do I do? In each case I can go to the web and find what I need. The information is usually in a PDF (Portable Document Format) file. A PDF file looks and prints just like the original paper document. Since I have a folder of Owners Manuals on my PC, I can easily find them and print any part of one that I need. When doing my taxes, I can print whichever form I need, fill it out, and send it in. There are a number of programs / apps on PC's and portable devices that read PDF files. Also, Microsoft Office and LibreOffice programs and others will save files in PDF format.

34: Misc.

This is the spot where I throw in some things that didn't seem to fit in other places.

Symbolically Speaking.

Symbols and icons have been used in print and on screens for quite some time. Recently one of my students pointed out that some of them are outdated and today's newer generation may not understand them. For example, take the telephone handset. How many kids have even seen one? Here are some examples.

Analog Computers

In this book I have used the term "computer" synonymously with "digital computer". Were there "analog computers"? Yes, let's talk about them. When I studied Electrical Engineering I used differential equations (a type of mathematics) to calculate the voltages and currents in an electrical circuit (one with resistors, capacitors, and inductors). Instead, if I built the electrical circuit and measured the voltages and currents, I could solve the differential equation. That's one type of analog computer. The advent of digital computing made simple analog computers obsolete although some are still around for specific applications.

Conclusion

Textbooks don't have conclusions. But, since this is my book, I am going to have one.

Some topics took a lot more words to describe than others. This does not necessarily imply that these topics are more important than some of the others. I may also mention certain systems or products. This does not necessarily imply that they are better than some of the others.

We have seen many examples of "One Size Doesn't Fit All". Printers was a prime example. With all the types of printers and features within each type, picking the one for you may involve some research, based on your specific needs. Operating Systems was another. If you use Windows, occasionally you may get an hourglass while you are trying to do something. It is a little annoying (maybe more), but you can live with it. Suppose you are pulling out onto the freeway with your new hybrid car (which contains lots of computers). You step on the gas and the car replies, "Wait a minute, I am updating my mileage calculations!" Not good! In portable devices like Smartphones and tablets, the choices are staggering.

With all of today's gadgets we understand how to work things, but not how they work. We live in a world of rapid change. By the time I publish this book, it will be out of date.

I am reminded of a meeting between a president of a large computer company and the president of a large automobile company. The computer company president commented, "If you had improved automobiles the way we improved computers they would get 200 miles a gallon and cost 10 dollars." The automobile company responded. "Yes, but who would want a car that crashes every few days!"

As some of you read the earlier sections, describing a primitive computer or device you may say, "I remember that", SORRY!

Well, this is the end, no homework, no quizes, no project, no final exam. My last question that I would ask my students, "Did you enjoy it and did you learn anything?"

I see that I have written over 30,000 words. I guess that my "Scope Creep" has crept.

Section 4: Then and Now

Glossary:

Application Software: Programs that perform something useful for a user.

BASIC: Beginner's All-purpose Symbolic Instruction Code. A general-purpose, high-level easy to use programming language created in 1964.Visual BASIC and GAMBAS are modern extensions of BASIC.

Bluetooth: A standard for the short-range wireless interconnection of mobile phones, computers, and other electronic devices. Its range is about 30 feet.

CARDIAC: The "CARDboard Illustrative Aid to Computation", a cardboard tool for teaching computer concepts.

Emulation: An **emulator** is hardware or software that enables one computer system (called the *host*) to behave like another computer system (called the *guest*).

ENIAC (**Electronic Numerical Integrator and Computer**): ENIAC was amongst the earliest electronic general-purpose computers made. It was designed and primarily used to calculate artillery firing tables for the United States Army's Ballistic Research Laboratory and put in use in 1946. ENIAC could calculate a trajectory that took a human 20 hours in 30 seconds.

FLOP: Floating-point operations per second. Floating-point operations are the computers equivalent of scientific notation (e.g. 6.02×10^{23}). Floating-point arithmetic requires more processing power than normal binary arithmetic.

FORTRAN: FORmula TRANslaton. A programming language developed by IBM in the 1950s for scientific and engineering applications. FORTRAN is still in use today and free downloads for PC's are available.

Section 4: Then and Now

GUI: Graphical User Interface: An interface that allows users to interact with computers and devices using icons and pictures instead of text.

Hardware: The circuitry that makes the computer work. The case, power supply, fans, etc. are also hardware.

Hexadecimal: A numbering system with 16 digits ("0" to "9" and "A" to "F"). Hexadecimal is used because it only takes one quarter of the number of digits to represent a number.

Icon: A small picture on a computer screen or document that represents a program or function.

IDE: Integrated Development Environment. A program that contains all the tools needed to develop programs (a form editing tool, a source code editor, a compiler, a debugger, and other tools).

Linux: An open source Operating System based on UNIX. It runs on PC's and the Raspberry Pi and C.H.I.P computers. It is also the basis for Android and Mac OS.

Local Area Network (LAN): A network that supports a group of computers and devices that are close to each other like an office, school, or home.

Octal: A numbering system similar to hexadecimal, but with only 8 digits. It was popular when some computers used 12, 24, and 36 bit words (4, 8, and 12 octal digits).

Operating System: An operating system (OS) is system software that manages computer hardware and software resources and provides common services for computer programs.

Mainframe Computer: A computer with large processing capability, used by large companies.

Section 4: Then and Now

Minicomputer: A computer of medium power, smaller and less expensive than a Mainframe.

Murphy's Law: An **adage** that states: "Anything that can go wrong will go wrong" (and usually at the worst time).

Optical Character Recognition (OCR): The identification of printed characters using a scanning device and software. It translates a picture of the characters into a text file.

Open Source: Software that is free to use and modify.

Packet: A package of information sent across the Internet. It contains data, the sending address, the destination address, and information used to assure the integrity of the packet when received.

Pixel: A picture element. The smallest addressable element in a picture.

Relational Database: A database where data is stored in one or more tables which can be related to other tables using key fields.

Software: The programs that are needed to make the computer do something. Software is divided into System Software (like the Operating System) and Application Software (the programs that do something useful for the user).

Supercomputer: A computer with extensive processing power.

System Software: An Operating System and any associated utility programs.

Virtual Machine: a *virtual machine* (VM) is an emulation of a computer system. Virtual machines are based on **computer architectures** and provide functionality of a physical computer.

VISIAC: A computer emulation of CARDIAC.

Wi-Fi: a wireless standard allowing computers, smartphones, or other devices to connect to the Internet or communicate with one another within a particular area. It has a typical range of about 100 feet.

WYSIWYG: "What You See Is what You Get." With a Graphical User Interface (GUI) the computer can display a document as it will look when it is printed (almost).

Appendices

Appendix 1: A Half adder

A half adder (see figure 2) is a simple computer logic circuit that adds two binary numbers. Here is how the logic in the half adder works:

If **A** is a "0" and **B** is a "0" then **S** is a "0" and C is a "0". Thus, "0" plus "0" = "0" with no carry into the next column. If **A** is "1" or **B** is "1" then **S** is a "1." "0" + "1" = "1" or "1" + "0" = "1" with no carry into the next column.

If **A** = "1" and **B** = "1" then **S** is a "0" with a carry. We have just designed what we call a half adder.

Appendix 2: The VISIAC emulator

The VISIAC emulator is written in Microsoft Visual Basic 2013 - a modern Integrated Development Environment (IDE) and programming language. It has 9 forms and over 1,200 lines of code. The main form was designed to look like CARDIAC as much as possible. It includes an assembler and debugging tools.

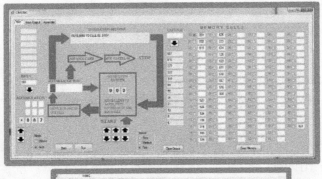

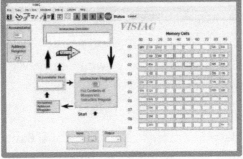

Figure 57: CARDIAC and VISIAC

There is also a VISIAC emulator written for Linux using the GAMBAS programming language / IDE. Many of the statements in GAMBAS are identical to those in Visual Basic, but some are slightly different, and a few are quite different.

Appendix 3: The VISIAC (CARDIAC) Instruction set

Opcode	Mnemonic	Operation
0	INP	Read a card into memory
1	CLA	Clear accumulator and add from memory (load)
2	ADD	Add from memory to accumulator
3	TAC	Test accumulator and jump if negative

Appendices

Opcode	Mnemonic	Operation
4	SFT	Shift accumulator
5	OUT	Write memory location to output card
6	STO	Store accumulator to memory
7	SUB	Subtract memory from accumulator
8	JMP	Jump and save PC
9	HRS	Halt and reset

INP

The INP instruction reads a single card from the input and stores the contents of that card into the memory location identified by the operand address. (MEM[a] ← INPUT)

CLA

This instruction causes the contents of the memory location specified by the operand address to be loaded into the accumulator. (ACC ← MEM[a])

ADD

The ADD instruction takes the contents of the accumulator, adds it to the contents of the memory location identified by the operand address and stores the sum into the accumulator. (ACC ← ACC + MEM[a])

TAC

The TAC instruction is VISIAC's only conditional branch instruction. It tests the accumulator, and if the accumulator is negative, then the PC is loaded with the operand address. Otherwise, the PC is not modified and the program continues with the instruction following the TAC. (If ACC < 0, PC ← a)

SFT

This instruction causes the accumulator to be shifted to the left by some number of digits and then back to the right some number of digits. The amounts by which it is shifted are shown above in the encoding for the SFT instruction. (ACC ← (ACC × 10^l) / 10^r)

OUT

The OUT instruction takes the contents of the memory location specified by the operand address and writes them out to an output card. (OUTPUT ← MEM[a])

STO

This is the inverse of the CLA instruction. The accumulator is copied to the memory location given by the operand address. (MEM[a] ← ACC)

SUB

In the SUB instruction the contents of the memory location identified by the operand address is subtracted from the contents of the accumulator and the difference is stored in the accumulator. (ACC ← ACC − MEM[a])

JMP

The JMP instruction first copies the PC into the operand part of the instruction at address 99. So if the VISIAC is executing a JMP instruction stored in memory location 42, then the value 843 will be stored in location 99. Then the operand address is copied into the PC, causing the next instruction to be executed to be the one at the operand address. (MEM[99] ← 800 + PC; PC ← a)

HRS

The HRS instruction halts the VISIAC and puts the operand address into the PC. (PC ← a; HALT)

Appendix 4: Tricks of the Trade

As people become familiar with the computer system they are using, they learn a few tricks that come in handy. Here are a few that I have learned. I will talk primarily about the current Microsoft Windows platform, although similar tricks apply to other platforms including Linux and Mac OS.

The most important "trick" is know how to get more information about a subject. As an example, I am not sure of exactly how to put a picture inside an Excel spreadsheet cell (putting one on a worksheet is easy). I know that it can be done and that it is complicated. What do I do? Go to the Internet! With a little of bit of searching I can find the detailed instructions of how to do it. I am almost always successful in finding what I need. It may take a bit of searching and some trial-and-error work to do what you want, but it is usually worth it.

Sometimes there is something on the screen (an image) that you would like to use in a document or a presentation. The "Snipping Tool" is ideal for this purpose. You simply run the tool and select the part of the screen you are interested in. It could be on something from another document or presentation or something on the web. Once you have selected it you can paste it anywhere or save it as an image file. I did this many times in creating this book.

When you copy or cut something it is saved in the Windows clipboard (a program). This clipboard has only one buffer and saves only the last item cut or copied. Some clipboards like the one in Microsoft Office can save more items. You can even copy and paste between platforms (to and from virtual machine O/S's like Linux and between a MAC-OS and a mobile device)

144

Often people would like to use more than one browser (I use Edge, Firefox and Chrome). Each has its own "bookmarks" (Edge calls them "Favorites"). I "export" the ones from my favorite browser to a file, then load another browser and "import" the file to have an exact copy of the bookmarks. This even works across platforms. My Linux systems also have the same bookmarks as my Windows ones.

Sometimes you would like to look at two windows on the screen simultaneously (like a word document and a web page). Open the first one and click on the "Max" (make sure it is already on the "Max" size) button to make the window normal size. Move it all the way to the left of the screen. The window should fill the left half of the screen. Select the second window and do the same, only moving it to the right of the screen. This method also works for Linux.

You may have a situation where you don't have enough free space on your main drive to fit everything you want (this may happen especially in newer computers where the main drive is an SSD device). You may have a lot of free space on another drive, one on your computer or an external one, but would like to have some items together. As an example, you want all your picture folders under: "Pictures". After you have moved the folder to the other drive, copy its folder name and paste it as a shortcut in the folder on your main drive. Just remember that the drive name of the other drive must be the same every time you mount it (this isn't a problem if both are internal drives).

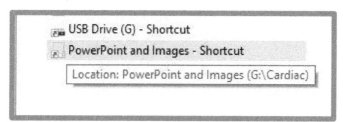

Appendices

Appendices

Appendix 5: Linux - Learn it and Love it

Linux, an operating system created by Linus Torvalds in 1991, deserves more attention. Linux is based on UNIX. I use Ubuntu, a Linux version based on the Debian architecture. It is usually run on personal computers and is not only free, but can be modified by users, since it is open source code. It also runs on the Raspberry Pi computer.

UNIX was developed by Bell Labs in the 1970's. It had a command driven interface and ran on a number of computers, including Digital Equipment Corporation's PDP series of minicomputer, as well as AT&T's 3B2 line of computers.

The most common way to get it is to download it from the web, burn a bootable DVD from it, then install it onto your computer, just like you would install Windows. You can replace the current O/S (making it the only O/S on your computer), add it to an existing O/S, or install in under a Virtual Machine. Be CAREFUL if you choose the second option, since you could wipe out your current O/S if you make a mistake.

When you load your release of Ubuntu you get a number of applications, including LibreOffice, the GIMP picture editor, a browser, and music and video players. It has a "Add, Remove, Update Software" menu item where you can select and download additional programs (many of them are free) and utilities to maintain and upgrade the system. It also retains the UNIX command line interface with the UNIX "Shell" and hundreds of commands, including man (as in manual) pages for the commands. It is NOT subject to malware like another O/S (which I won't mention here).

For people who may want to try some programming, it has GAMBAS and Python IDE's. GAMBAS in a "Visual Basic like" Integrated Development Environment (IDE). It has most of the

147

screen objects (like text boxes, buttons and menu's) that Microsoft Windows has. I found the transition from Visual Basic to GAMBAS to be a reasonable one. In fact, I even have a GAMBAS version of VISIAC.

Tables

Figures

Appendices

Appendices

151

Appendices

INDEX

Appendices

153

About the Author

Marc Lipman spent his career in the field of computers — having seen them grow (shrink) from multimillion2 dollar room sized devices to handheld ones of equivalent power, occasionally teaching at the college and corporate level.

As a sidelight he occasionally wrote items for publication in publications ranging from "Commodore" magazine to "Bridge" magazine. He still writes. He is a frequent contributor to the Sandpaper, the weekly newspaper for Long Beach Island.

After "retiring", he pursued a number of hobbies and activities ranging from kayaking to duplicate bridge to softball to being a grandfather. He is currently an adjunct professor at a county college and a docent at the Barnegat Light Museum.

I wish to thank Lauren Lipman (my daughter-in-law) for her extensive work in editing this document and making important suggestions!

Other books by Marc Lipman*

Fiction

The Sandpaper Stories

Power to The People

And Now for Something Completely Different

Non-Fiction

Photo Phinishing

* Also available as E-Books